A

THE CHARLES A. HART
MEMORIAL LECTURES 1968

Theology and the Future

THE CHARLES A. HART
MEMORIAL LECTURES 1968

Theology
and the Future

E. L. MASCALL

*Professor of Historical Theology in the
University of London, Priest of the Oratory of the Good Shepherd*

Darton, Longman & Todd

First published in Great Britain in 1968 by
Darton, Longman & Todd Ltd
64 Chiswick High Road, London W4
© 1968 Dr E. L. Mascall
Printed in Great Britain by
Balding & Mansell, London and Wisbech

232 51011 3

Acknowledgements

The author and publishers make acknowledgement with thanks to James Nisbet & Company Limited for extracts from PROSPECT FOR THEOLOGY, *Essays in Honour of H. H. Farmer*. To Collins Publishers for extracts from FROM ANATHEMA TO DIALOGUE by Roger Garaudy. To Longmans, Green & Co Limited for extracts from CORPUS CHRISTI by Dr E. L. Mascall.

Contents

Foreword

The lectures contained in this book were delivered in March 1968 at the Catholic University of America in Washington, D.C., on the foundation established by the bequest of the Right Reverend Monsignor Charles A. Hart for courses of lectures by visiting scholars in the fields of philosophy and theology. For almost all his working life Monsignor Hart was a member of the Faculty of Philosophy in the University and for many years he held the office of Professor. By all who knew him he was esteemed as an exemplary priest, a devoted friend and an erudite and dedicated scholar. It is typical of the broad-minded and ecumenical spirit animating Catholic University that its invitation to give the first series of Charles A. Hart Memorial Lectures should have been extended to one who is an Englishman and an Anglican. To all those who made my visit to Washington both enjoyable and profitable it gives me great pleasure to express my gratitude for their many kindnesses.

The five lectures included under the heading "The Future of Christian Theology" were given on five successive weekdays. The sixth lecture, entitled "Theology of the Secular" was given to a wider audience on a Sunday afternoon.   E.L.M.

THE FUTURE OF
CHRISTIAN THEOLOGY

CHAPTER ONE

The Task of the Theologian

THE TITLE WHICH I HAVE CHOSEN FOR THIS course of lectures might suggest that they are intended as an exercise in the activity of prophecy. That is not my intention. Prophecy is always a hazardous business, unless one can be assured of a share in the foreknowledge of God, though there are two ways in which one can avoid the more immediate personal inconveniences of being a false prophet. One way is to invest one's utterances with a character of oracular ambiguity, like the computer in the story, which, when asked "Will the Republicans or the Democrats win the election?" replied "Yes", and when confronted with the further question "Yes, what?" replied "Yes, please". The other way is to project one's prophecies so far into the future that one will be dead before they can be either verified or falsified. In any case, people can become very skilful in the game of cheating the prophet, as Gilbert Keith Chesterton pointed out in *The Napoleon of Notting Hill*, even if, as happened in that story, they are driven to the desperate expedient of leaving things exactly as they were. In matters affecting the life and thought of the Church, prophecy is very specially precarious, for in these, more than in other matters, the prophet, however sensitive he may be in reading the signs of the times,

B

may be refuted by the unheralded intervention of God. To be convinced of this, one need only cast one's mind back to the days before Pope John XXIII and ask oneself how much anyone was then able to foresee of the condition of the post-Conciliar Roman Catholic Church.

What I shall attempt might better be described as programme than as prophecy, though even the word "programme" may suggest something more systematic and detailed than I am likely to achieve. All I shall venture to do is to indicate some of the themes and procedures which I believe the theologian of today should have as his concern if he is to be as useful as possible to the Church and the world in the not too distant future.

I do not believe that the task of the theologian today is essentially different from his task at any other epoch. It is to help the Church to acquire a deeper understanding of the Christian faith and to mediate, interpret and commend that faith to the contemporary world. But here a good deal of preliminary clarification is needed.

First, we must distinguish theology in the strict sense, as the study of God and of created beings in their relation to God, from the vast number of other studies which are commonly included in the term "theology" in modern universities and which, while they have a valuable ancillary function in relation to theology proper, have a perfectly legitimate status as secular studies in their own right. To quote what I have said elsewhere, in my inaugural lecture at King's College London:

> In the wider sense Theology includes a vast range of disciplines in which scholars apply to the documents, monuments, events and behavioral patterns of Judaism and Christianity the same techniques and criteria that other scholars apply to the documents, monuments, events and behavioral patterns of other movements of human thought and culture: Old-Testament History, the Literary Criticism of the Bible, Biblical Archaeology, Ecclesiastical History, Liturgiology, the Psychology of Religion, the Philosophy of Religion and so on. . . . They provide material of the utmost value for the consideration of the Biblical and dogmatic theologian; I need only mention as examples of this the way in which recent work on the Qumran scrolls and the Gnostic codices has thrown light upon the precise nature of primitive Christianity and in which the work of liturgical scholars has assisted our understanding of the character of the Christian Eucharist. Where these disciplines differ from Theology in the strict sense is in the fact that, while they are concerned with the Christian religion as a phenomenon for study, they do not appeal to the Christian revelation for either their techniques or their criteria. . . . The Old-Testament historian, the Biblical critic, the ecclesiastical historian, the liturgical scholar scrutinise and

evaluate the events of Jewish history, the authorship and composition of the books of the Bible, the often sordid and unedifying episodes of the Church's past and the behaviour of Christians at worship with the same ruthless and impartial objectivity with which other scholars investigate the history of ancient China, the provenance of the Rig Veda and the Upanishads, the development and ramifications of Buddhism and the ritual performances of the Aztecs.[1]

In contrast with this, the Christian theologian, in the strict sense of the term, while he will make plentiful use of these ancillary disciplines and may on occasion even indulge in them himself, believing as he must that grace perfects nature and does not destroy it, will see his own proper task as the elucidation and the deepening of the Church's understanding of the faith from within the Church's tradition of life, thought and worship. The basic fact about the Christian theologian is that he is a member of the Body of Christ and, within that Body, a member of the great historical tradition of Christian thinkers. If this assertion should sound anti-rational and obscurantist it is well to recall that a number of scholars have pointed out that something very like this is true of the positive sciences. A man does not become a physicist by getting himself trained in something called the scientific method and then applying it to one chosen

[1] *Theology and History*, p. 4.

class of physical objects and occurrences. He does it by entering into a community of physicists, living with them, thinking with them, and arguing with them, and his expertise as a physicist will be acquired and developed in the process. Both Dr Michael Polanyi and Dr William G. Pollard, to name only two, have laid emphasis upon this fact; so, from a slightly different angle, has Fr Bernard Lonergan.[1] Important as this is for the scientist, it is, I believe, even more important for the theologian, but in the latter case the matter is vastly more complex. For, if the theologian believes that the Christian faith is true and is himself a practising Christian, he is not only a member of the community of theologians but is also a member of the Christian Church; he will be theologising not from outside but from inside the Revelation, the Church and the Faith. Furthermore, the community to which he belongs includes not only those Christians who are on earth but those who are beyond the grave as well. Denis de Rougemont is quoted[2] as saying, in *The Devil's Share*, that the penalty for not knowing the history of Christian theology is to have to make the same mistakes all over again. The Christian theologian is, however, not confined to reading the writings of his forbears; through his membership of the Body he is in living communion with them. This does not mean, therefore, that the theologian

[1] M. Polanyi, *Personal Knowledge*; W. G. Pollard, *Physicist and Christian*; B. J. F. Lonergan, *Insight*, p. 705.
[2] Harold O. J. Brown, *Christianity Today*, 15 April 1966, p. 4.

should always be looking to the past in an attitude that is simply antiquarian or archaeological; quite the contrary. And this brings me to my second point.

Anyone who believes that the Christian religion has an urgent concern with the aspirations and problems of men and women today can hardly fail to be disturbed by the disproportionate extent to which, in many countries, the energy of theologians and of theological faculties is diverted – presumably to the satisfaction of the scholars themselves – into studies which are only in the remotest sense theological. In the English journal *Theology* of September 1965 there were published the findings of a survey made by Dr E. J. Burge, a physicist at King's College, London, of those theses which succeeded in obtaining higher degrees in the theological faculties of the British Isles from 1950 to 1962 inclusive. Out of 751 theses listed, only 116 – less than one-sixth – were classified under the heading "Theological Thought". No less than 307 were devoted to Church History and Biography. Old Testament and New Testament together added up to 107, 19 were on the Philosophy of Religion, 58 on the Comparative Study of Religions, 17 on Liturgical Studies and eight on Ethics. It is, of course, only fair to recognise that Biblical studies might be not only historical and critical but also theological, and that even the biography of a Christian thinker could hardly avoid paying some attention to his Christian thinking. Nevertheless the picture is sufficiently alarming, not only because of the comparatively small place occupied by Theological Thought but also because of the quite minimal place occupied by Philosophy of Religion, Ethics and the Comparative Study of Religions, all of which might be considered of some importance in a world in which both belief and behaviour are becoming increasingly secularised and in which men of different nations and cultures have become aware of one another as never before. Whether anything comparable to this spread of the different disciplines which gratefully huddle under the ample and hospitable umbrella of theology in Britain is typical of other countries I do not know, but perhaps the example of the British Isles may serve as a dreadful warning.

I must, however, make one point clear. I do not think it is a bad thing for the clergy or members of religious orders to be engaged in secular academic pursuits. Apart from the contribution which they may be able to make to the welfare of the human race, both material and cultural, their own mental vision may be widened and deepened and they may be in a better position to understand the relation of the secular concern of man to the sacral. But if they are engaged in secular pursuits they ought not to delude themselves with the belief that they are doing theology. History does not become a branch of theology simply because most of the people with whom it is dealing happen to be clergymen, so that when Brutus stabs Caesar we have history *tout simple*, while if Bishop X poisons Cardinal Y we have ecclesiastical history, which is a branch of theology. History and biography are legitimate and praiseworthy enterprises, but they are not theology. And even the study of a Christian thinker's theology is not theology if it is a purely descriptive study and makes no attempt to assess his place within the Christian tradition and his contribution to its development. The theologian has indeed a duty to the secular order, but it does not consist of engaging in secular studies and labelling the activity "theology". It consists in furthering what I have elsewhere called "a theology of the secular", that is to say of applying the insights and criteria of the Christian faith to the secular concerns of man in order to illuminate, direct and transform them.

Christian theology should thus have an intense concern with all human activities, both sacral and secular, a concern which is quite distinct from the acquisition and practice of their several techniques. In developing an adequate theology of the secular the theologian will be immensely helped if he has an inside knowledge of some at least of those techniques, but to acquire and practise the techniques is not to do theology. And in a world as highly differentiated and specialised as the world of today it will hardly be possible for the theologian to make an adequate and relevant contribution to the theology of the secular if he associates only with other theologians. This is particularly true in the realm of what might be called "biological ethics", in which a theological judgment is demanded on certain human activities on which such a judgment has never been demanded before for the simple reason that the activities in question have only recently become possible. This includes such matters as the modification of human genetic material by microsurgical and other manipulation, the influencing of brain-processes by chemical, electrical and surgical means, the transplantation of bodily organs from one person to another and the separation of procreation from sexual intercourse, to name but a few. In 1963 and 1966 the CIBA Foundation published reports of conferences held under its auspices in which these and other problems were discussed by biologists, sociologists, lawyers, medical men and other specialists, including, significantly, two theologians, whose contributions were clearly felt to be relevant.[1] Much of this kind of sympathetic and cooperative discussion is needed for the development of a really intelligent theology of the secular, which will enable Christian leaders to speak on secular matters when they ought to speak, without speaking nonsense.

This, I must now make plain, does not imply that theology, if it is to be authentic and legitimate, must devote its efforts simply to the production of detailed and unambiguous pronouncements on the problems with which the contemporary world is confronted; that it should give up speculating about the Trinity, the hypostatic union and the Eucharistic sacrifice and

[1] *Man and his Future*, 1963; *Ethics in Medical Progress*, 1966.

give instead slick directives about Viet Nam, contraceptives, Rhodesia and monetary policy. I do not deny that the Church and its thinkers should be intimately involved in all that concerns human welfare; on the contrary I hold that they have an inescapable duty in this sphere. But if the Church's judgment and influence are to be in any way different from those of any decent and thoughtful humanist, if, that is, the Church is to have any contribution to offer that cannot be equally well made without her assistance, that contribution must arise from the specific insights that the Christian revelation gives into the nature, condition and resources of human beings. It must derive from those fundamental truths whose interpretation and exploration is the business of Christian theology. It is precisely because, on so many occasions in the past, the Church's leaders and spokesmen have been lacking in this theological insight that they have conceived their duty in the social sphere as simply consisting in lending the weight of religious rhetoric and religious emotion to the independently determined objectives of the social community of their own nation or class. The record which religious leaders in all countries have acquired by their utterances in time of war provides the most glaring example of the condition to which Christian witness can be reduced when it is not informed by an independently conceived theological judgment; the alternative to such a judgment is inevitably mere social conformity. Perhaps an even more terrible example is given by the way in which, in the days of colonial expansion, the nations professing Christianity so identified the mission of the Church with their own political and economic interests that today, in one country after another, as independence is achieved, the Christian faith itself is denounced as the discredited and superseded instrument and ally of the haves in their exploitation of the have-nots. In the words of Fr Van den Hout, quoted by Cardinal Suenens in his book *The Nun in the World*:

Our western civilisation has failed in its primary mission. A Christian civilisation, it could and should have christianised the universe. Deeply apostate, it sought only to exploit the universe for purely worldly, even basely materialistic ends. But if the white races have been able to enrich themselves to an unbelievable degree, it has been at the price of enormous and terrible social injustices. Its cornering of wealth, its creation of an immense proletariat, its culpable lack of concern in the face of the appalling misery of millions and hundreds of millions of human beings undernourished and dying of starvation, have aroused and built up an enormous rancour that falls easy prey to the apostles of human pseudo-liberty.[1]

A more up-to-date example of the same tendency, and one which is more insidious because it is often combined with a real compassion for the underprivileged, is

[1] op. cit., p. 152.

seen in the demand of the "radical" or "secularising" school of theologians that the Church shall conform its thinking and speaking to the outlook of secularist western technocracy.

The necessary condition for a genuinely Christian social consciousness in the Church is the existence of a vigorous and responsible activity of theological thought and discussion concerned with the truths about God and man on the basis of which alone a Christian judgment can be formed. It is the failure to achieve this that accounts for the otherwise puzzling phenomenon of religious spokesmen who simultaneously denounce the Church for its supine conformity to the social contexts and currents of the past and demand that it shall conform to the social contexts and currents of the part of the world in which they themselves live today. As long ago as 1939 Dr Vigo A. Demant drew attention to the fact that when men reject belief in a transcendent Reality on which their very existence depends, "some aspect of man's life in the actual historic process slyly insinuate[s] itself into the position of the displaced transcendent".

The whole modern world [he writes] in those aspects of it which really affect the lives of men, is a field of conflict between various forms of demonism, as we may call the attempts to give some element in the temporal order the absolute value which only belongs to the transcendent. . . . Religious teachers, who alone are the guardians of the truth of a transcendent reality, which truth is the only guarantor of the truth of being, have largely succumbed to the prevailing dogma in spite of doctrinal allegiances to the contrary. In purely moral terms they identify their religious position with one form of the dogma of becoming, be it Liberalism or Totalitarianism, according to their dislike of the practical results of the opposite number in the same dogmatic frame of reference.[1]

The choice today may not be between Liberalism and Totalitarianism, or at least not between the forms in which they were respectively manifested in the nineteen-thirties, but I believe that Dr Demant's diagnosis is no less valid today. In the theological context, the clearest example of this tendency to absolutise what is essentially relative is to be seen, as I have already suggested, in the more extreme instances of secularised theology, which do openly and avowedly what their predecessors did unconsciously and unreflectively.

I would therefore maintain that the Church can bear a healthy and intelligent witness to her Gospel only if behind this there lives a healthy and intelligent activity of what we might call "pure theology", an activity of theologising which, while its practitioners will be conscious of its practical implications and consequences, is pursued for its own sake, or at least for no other sake

[1] *The Religious Prospect*, pp. 68f.

than that of truth and of God. This may well sound like the self-interested plea of a professional, who is anxious to secure a foothold for himself in a world that is hostile or indifferent to theologians. I would therefore point out that there is a very close parallel in the very different realm of the positive sciences. "Most of the greatest discoveries, such as the discovery of electricity, X-rays, radium and atomic energy", writes Dr W. I. B. Beveridge, "originated from pure research, which allows the worker to follow unexpected, interesting clues without the intention of achieving results of practical value."[1] We might also adduce the way in which the most abstruse and "useless" branches of pure mathematics have a way of suddenly and unexpectedly becoming "applied" when some branch of physics delightedly discovers them lying ready for use. Such were, for instance, the entry of the tensor calculus into relativity-theory and of group-theory into quantum- and fundamental-particle physics. I have no use for the theological Philistinism which despises any discussion whose immediate practical utility is not evident. There is, I believe, great need for theological thinking of a type that will seem to many to be abstract and theoretical, though I would not myself use those adjectives to describe the study of the living God. Talk *about* abstractions is very abstract, but so, as Fr Karl Rahner has reminded us, is talk about "the concrete" as such, for "the concrete", like "the abstract", is itself an

[1] *The Art of Scientific Investigation*, p. 126

abstraction.[1] The proper use of abstractions is for talking about concrete realities, and no reality is, in this sense, more concrete than God. It is not because there has been too much "pure theology" that "applied theology" has often lost its link with the real world, but because there has been too little. It is, of course, true that theology has sometimes got lost in an alembicated realm of logic and linguistics in which, to quote Rabelais' satirical example, it finds itself discussing whether a chimaera bombinating in a vacuum can eat second intentions. But, once again, the cure for bad theology is good theology, not no theology; and it is certainly not non-theological studies claiming the title of theology.

I said at the beginning of this lecture that the theologian's task is to help the Church to acquire a deeper understanding of the Christian faith and to mediate, interpret and commend that faith to the contemporary world. He is thus poised between the two poles of the faith and the world and is in an extremely delicate position. If he is over-anxious for the integrity of the faith, he may fail altogether to communicate it to the world; like the servant in the parable, he will be so frightened of losing his Master's money that he will bury it in a hole in the earth. If, on the other hand, all his attention and effort are devoted to discovering how to communicate with the contemporary world, he may find that he has succeeded in communicating something,

[1] *The Dynamic Element in the Church*, p. 35.

but not the Christian faith; most probably he will be handing back to the world its own beliefs and assumptions adorned with a Christian label. We have seen both these excesses in recent years. The disciples of Dr Karl Barth have in effect denied that the world has any capacity of hearing and receiving the faith at all; for them the Church's sole task is to proclaim the Word of God in Biblical terms, leaving God to decide whether, with the Word, he will give the power to accept it. At the other extreme, the secularist or "radical" theologians who are so vociferous today assert that the faith, in anything like its traditional form, is hopelessly incommunicable to modern men and women and insist that the Church must take the contemporary outlook as it stands and adjust the Gospel to it. As so often happens with opposite extremes, both these positions rest on the same basic assumption: that there is an irreconcilable incompatibility between the traditional faith and the modern world. Nor will either of them accept the mediating position of Paul Tillich, for whom the world asks the questions and the faith gives the answers; since the Barthians will maintain that the world cannot ask the right questions and the secularist theologians will insist that the faith, in anything like its traditional form, cannot give intelligible answers. Clearly we are here confronted with some of the fundamental problems of Christian theology, the problems of the relation between reason and revelation, between nature and grace, and, in the last resort, between man and God. Here I can only state my own position, which I believe to be that of the central Christian tradition in both East and West and which was plainly expressed by Pope John in his inaugural address to the Second Vatican Council, that "the substance of the ancient doctrine, contained in the 'deposit of faith', is one thing; its formulation is quite another".

To pronounce such a formula as this is not to close discussion. It may be by no means easy in any particular case to decide whether two different formulas express the same substance of doctrine or not; but then, as Fr Karl Rahner has remarked, "even in theology [I would almost say 'especially in theology'] to settle one question, even correctly, raises three new questions that remain to be settled."[1] The Church is no stranger to this kind of situation. It occurred, to give one instance, in the third century, when it had to be settled whether, when Dionysius of Alexandria used the formula "three *hypostases* and one *ousia*" to describe the Holy Trinity, he was expressing the same basic doctrine as was Dionysius of Rome, who used the formula "three *personae* and one *substantia*". And although it was in the end agreed that both *were* expressing the same basic doctrine, neither Greeks nor Latins have ever supposed that the others conceived it in exactly the same way as themselves.

There are, of course, many difficult philosophical problems about the meanings of sentences and their

[1] *The Dynamic Element in the Church*, p. 76.

C

relation to reality. It would not be appropriate to discuss them here. What I must stress, however, is that the Christian theologian is the inheritor of a tradition to which he is bound to pay the deepest respect, if only because it embodies the life and thought of countless Christian men and women many of whom were no less intelligent and holy than he. And in making his own contribution to the tradition there are a number of norms by which he should be guided.

First of all, just because it is difficult to know exactly where to draw the line between the substance of the doctrine and its formulation, the theologian should be very tentative in his assertions and very ready to submit them to the judgment of his fellow Christians. The rash way in which many scholars in the past were accustomed to attach to their most recent hypotheses the label "Assured Results of Modern Scholarship" is generally condemned today even by those who are most inclined to attach the same label to theirs. On the other hand, provided he is prepared to put forth his hypotheses *as* hypotheses, the theologian should feel free to speculate within the broadest limits set by common sense and utility. Indeed, unless the theologian is prepared to take this hypothetical attitude towards even his brightest ideas, it is difficult to see how he can have the benefit of any judgment other than his own. And it is important to add that, if the theologian should be under very little external discipline, it is all the more (and not, as some appear to imagine, all the less) incumbent upon him to exercise considerable restraint upon himself.

It would be widely agreed today, both within and without the Roman Communion, that until the Second Vatican Council produced its impact, Roman Catholic scholars were commonly subjected to a discipline that was excessive in its requirements and often unjust in its exercise. Today this is very largely a thing of the past, and the great majority of Roman Catholic theologians appear to be as free to speculate as anyone else. It is not surprising if this newly found freedom is sometimes abused. I would therefore appeal to them, as to those of other communions who have long enjoyed this freedom, to take very seriously the obligation of self-discipline to which I have just referred. The theologian, like other scholars, has an obligation to truth which is imperative and categorical. This does not entitle him to claim the authority of immutable truth for his own conclusions, however plausible they may seem to him to be. The path of theological scholarship (and of other types of scholarship as well) is strewn with the ruins of theories which in their time seemed so well-founded that anyone who ventured to question them was either viewed with pity as feeble-minded or with indignation as a dangerous obscurantist. The theologian might well profit by the example of the mathematician and philosopher Alfred North Whitehead, who, when he was urged to accept as the final truth about the universe the new theories of relativity and quanta which had deposed the Newtonian physics from two and a half centuries of unchallenged supremacy, replied, "I have been fooled once, and I'll be damned if I'll be fooled again."[1]

Respect for tradition does not, of course, imply that the tradition itself may not at times suffer from loss of direction or of vitality. Dr J. P. Mackey has shown how, in J. B. Franzelin and his followers, tradition became virtually identified with the magisterium, so that study of its life-history was virtually ignored since the contemporary magisterium was always at hand for consultation.[2]

Again, the disastrous view of tradition and Scripture as two independent sources of doctrine, which became universal from the fourteenth century onwards until its dislodgment in the Decree on Revelation of the Second Vatican Council, did much to fossilise the notion of tradition and to lead the theologian to view his task as little more than the deduction of conclusions, by the method of the syllogism, from propositions given, in whole or in part, by revelation. How refreshing it is to turn to such an admirable product of post-Conciliar thought as Brother Gabriel Moran's *Theology of Revelation*, with its superb concept of the human mind of the ascended and glorified Christ as the place where the perfect revelation of the Father is contained is one unified act of contemplation and is

[1] *Dialogues of Alfred North Whitehead as recorded by Lucien Price*, p. 345.
[2] *The Modern Theology of Tradition*, passim; *Life and Grace*, ch. iii.

thence communicated to Christ's body the Church, and to its members, according to their need and condition. I shall, I think, be following Brother Moran's line of thought if I describe the development of Christian doctrine as a progressive translation, into the conceptual and linguistic framework of our earthly modes of knowing and speaking, of one aspect after another of the truth contained in the mind of Christ, who is himself the Truth and the Word of the Father.

I have just said that the tradition itself may suffer at times from a loss of direction and vitality, and one of the ways in which this may be manifested is in the treatment of formulations and outlooks which are, in fact, peripheral to the tradition and of only relative and transient significance as if they were part of the unchanging and inadmissible deposit of faith. Here one is treading on ecumenically dangerous ground, but, to take only one instance, it has become clear quite recently that many pronouncements of curial origin which had been treated as in practice, if not necessarily in theory, as final and irreformable are legitimately open to critical, and indeed drastic, reconsideration. If it is not so easy to point to examples in other Christian bodies, the reason may be that those bodies have not in recent years subjected themselves to such a radical self-scrutiny as that to which the Roman Communion subjected itself at Vatican II. It does not seem possible to maintain that the promise of the Lord to his Church, that the Spirit of truth would guide it into all truth, is incompatible with continual vacillations from the strait and narrow way; nor should this surprise us if we remember that the grace of God respects and does not annihilate the freedom he has given us. I would suggest that the guidance of the Spirit within the Church may be conceived as analogous to the cybernetic or "negative feed-back" controls which have become so familiar to us today, and which, while they do not prevent the behaviour of a machine or an organism from varying from the normal and balanced condition, correct the variations and restore the norm, so that there is never a complete collapse into chaos and the purpose of the machine or organism is maintained. If so mechanical an analogy seems inappropriate we may remember that our bodies were full of cybernetic controls long before we recognised their existence or applied the principle to machines.

It is also important to recognise that verbal formulas in which Christian truths are expressed are inevitably subject to the limitations of all human language, besides raising difficulties of their own. Their own special problems arise from the inherent inadequacy of human language to express transcendent and divine realities, and I need not remind you how much thought has been put into this problem, from the medievals with their doctrine of analogy to the philosophers and theologians of the present day. Here I can only affirm in passing that we *can* make intelligible statements about the divine mysteries whether we can satisfactorily account for this or not.[1] What I must emphasise now is that to understand correctly the meaning of any statement, whether theological or not, we must take care to see it in the context of its original utterance. In particular, when we are concerned with a statement of orthodox doctrine, it is essential to take account of the errors, if any, against which it was directed. A statement emphasising the duality of the human and divine natures in Christ, for example, will have very different nuances of meaning according as it was pronounced against a background of Nestorian, Eutychian or Chalcedonian Christology. And just as, in different contexts, the same verbal statement may have different meanings, so also, in different contexts, different verbal statements may have the same meaning. Thus it appears from discussions held in 1964 and 1967 between theologians of the "dyophysite" and "monophysite" Eastern churches that, whatever may or may not have been the case in the fifth, sixth and seventh centuries, there is no essential difference between their respective Christologies today.[2] Attention to theological minutiae does not necessarily produce schisms; it may also heal them.

A further consequence of this attention to context is that, however useful collections of extracts from doctrinal documents may be, they can be misleading if the

[1] Cf. my *Existence and Analogy* and *Words and Images* for fuller discussion of this point.

[2] Cf. *St. Vladimir's Seminary Quarterly* (Crestwood, N.Y.), VIII (1964), XI (1967).

passages which they contain are read simply in the theological context of the present day or, still more, if they are treated as having no contextual relation at all and as being supra-temporal manifestations of eternal truth. (Behold the greatness and the wretchedness of Denzinger!) In saying this I do not suggest that there can be no such thing as objective truth in either the doctrinal or any other realm; what I am pointing out is that linguistic statements, however august and authoritative they may be, can only approximate to it. The approximation may, of course, be very close indeed, and it may be amply sufficient to enable the mind to identify and grasp not merely the statement but the reality to which it refers. Language is not useless because it is not perfectly isomorphic with reality, though it would appear from the mathematical theory of the infinite that even finite reality is far richer than language can be. To take this further would require a discussion of the nature and the media of authority in matters of doctrine in the course of which denominational differences would be deeply involved and I do not propose to raise them here. I hope nevertheless that we may agree in recognising the inevitable element of relativity in doctrinal statements which arises from the inherent limitations of language as such, and I would suggest that a closer attention to their contextual setting might remove at least some of the differences which divide us. It is indeed largely through the adoption of this approach that the remarkable *rapprochement* has

taken place in recent years between Catholic and Protestant scholars on the sacrificial character of the
Eucharist, and that Dr Hans Küng and Dr Karl Barth
have found themselves in agreement on the hitherto
explosive issue of Justification.[1] I made considerable, if
largely implicit, use of this approach in my book *The
Recovery of Unity*, though I must admit that a good deal
of that work has been short-circuited by Vatican II.

To summarise, I have tried in this lecture to expound
and defend the view that the task of the theologian is to
help the Church to acquire a deeper understanding of
the Christian faith and to mediate, interpret and commend that faith to the contemporary world. I have also
tried to show that this view is neither introverted nor
obscurantist, but that on the contrary it enables him to
face the world of which he is part with understanding,
appreciation and discrimination. How far he is successful in this task it is not for him to judge, but it is
with this intention in mind that in the rest of this course
I shall try to consider the future of Christian theology.

[1] Cf. E. L. Mascall, *Corpus Christi*, 2nd ed., chs. iv-vi; H. Küng,
Justification, passim.

CHAPTER TWO

The Question of God

THE QUESTION OF GOD IS CLEARLY OF PRIMARY importance in Christian theology. Even the "death-of-God" theologians would agree about this, and indeed some of them proclaim the death of God with a vigour and enthusiasm which might well put to shame some of the theologians who believe that God is still alive. "If ours is truly a history in which God is no longer present", Dr Altizer insists, "then we are called upon not simply to accept the death of God with stoic fortitude but rather to will the death of God with the passion of faith."
He is not prepared to accept Dr Martin Buber's phrase "the eclipse of God".[1] "Such language", he writes, "betrays a nostalgia for a time that is past or a yearning for a future which is not yet present." And again: "To speak the name of God in a time of his withdrawal is nothing less than blasphemy, a blasphemy that profanes the holiness of God and makes a mockery of a faith that once gave witness to his presence."[2] Such "creative negation in theology" – the phrase is Dr Altizer's own – more than suggests a certain background anxiety that, although God is dead, he cannot

---

[1] M. Buber, *Eclipse of God* (1952).
[2] T. J. J. Altizer, "Creative Negation in Theology", in *Frontline Theology*, ed. D. Peerman, pp. 81, 82.

be relied upon to remain lying down unless we continually go on willing that he shall; and the assertion
that a non-existent God is offended if men presump-
tuously speak his name makes one tremble both for Dr
Altizer's metaphysics and for his sense of humour. He
makes it quite plain that it is God himself who is dead
and not merely our belief in him or our concern with
him; yet he apparently holds that whether God is alive
or dead depends entirely upon whether we will his
existence or not. Who "we" are is never explicitly
stated, but the implication is that "we" are men and
women who live in the technopolis of the nineteen-
sixties; and the picture that is evoked is that of a tug-of-
war between two teams, one consisting of a vast multi-
tude of thoroughly contemporary men and women,
willing with all their might that God should remain
dead, and the other of a small group of effete, nostalgic
and depressed left-overs, hoping against hope that God
might come to life again some day. It is true that Dr
Altizer's close associate Dr William Hamilton tells us
that "Death of God is, after all, a myth",[1] but the
point is that for these extreme "radicals" nothing, not
even God, exists except in so far as men believe that it
does and will that it shall. It is not really surprising that
the three muses who have inspired Dr Altizer's epic are
Hegel, with his doctrine of the Absolute Idea, Blake,
with his identification of Christ with Satan, and Nietz-

[1] "A Note on Radical Theology", in *Concilium*, IX, iii (Nov.
1967), p. 43.

sche, with his glorification of the naked will and his proclamation of the death of God.[1] Thus Dr Altizer can tell us that "God has actually died in Christ, that this death is both a historical and a cosmic event, and, as such, it is a final and irrevocable event, which cannot be reversed by a subsequent religious or cosmic movement",[2] thus implying that God has been dead ever since the Crucifixion. But he can also write such a passage as the following, which implies that the death of God has taken place only in our time:

> We are not simply saying that modern man is incapable of believing in God, or that modern culture is an idolatrous flight from the presence of God, or even that we exist in a time in which God has chosen to be silent. . . . A theological statement that proclaims the death of God must mean that God is not present in the Word of faith. Insofar as the theologian speaks of the death of God – and actually means what he speaks – he is speaking of the death of God himself. He is saying that because God has disappeared from history he is no longer present for faith. But he is truly absent, he is not simply hidden from view, and therefore he is truly dead. Once we can accept the death of God as a final and irrevocable event, then we can open ourselves to the full actuality of our history as an epiphany of the Word of faith.[3]

[1] T. J. J. Altizer, *The Gospel of Christian Atheism*, passim.
[2] ibid., p. 103.   [3] *Frontline Theology*, p. 82.

I would not venture to accuse Dr Altizer of complete consistency in these two passages, still less to maintain that the various "radical" theologians share as much of a common position as they appear to suppose. But I think we can see how it is possible for Dr Altizer to believe that God has been dead ever since the Crucifixion and also that his death has become a reality only in our own time, when men have, as he hopes and trusts, at last become able both to believe that God is dead and to will it. It is possible because Dr Altizer holds a purely subjective view of reality; because he assumes without argument a particular and very debatable metaphysic, a metaphysic, moreover, which is not specially characteristic of present-day philosophers. I think we can also see the answer to the question which must have puzzled many people, namely whether the radical Christian can see any need for prayer and, if so, what the content of his prayer must be. Clearly for him the highest form of prayer will consist of a unified and all-absorbing act of contemplation, in which he will, at one and the same time, be tranquilly accepting the death of God with his intellect and vehemently affirming it and rejoicing in it with his will.

I would gladly say no more about the radical theologians, for there is a more positive task which I wish to attempt. I must, however, devote some space to them, if only in order to indicate that I am acquainted with their views, impressed by them and quite unconvinced by them. I do not hold that God's existence depends in any way upon our belief in it or our acceptance of it, though I do hold that it is highly desirable that we should believe in it and accept it. I do not believe that the existence of any being depends on our belief in it or on our acceptance of it, not even the existence of ourselves. I do not admit that it is impossible for a sincere, intelligent and mature Christian today to believe in the existence of God in the traditional sense, for I know a number of sincere, intelligent and mature Christians who believe in it. I do not know for certain what is the correct diagnosis of the widespread unconcern with God in the modern world, though I do not think it is surprising, in a period when the development of scientific technology has directed man's mind towards the amazing things that he can do with the world and away from the God who sustains it. I do not know whether, as God sees it, there is less genuine religion in the world of today, when the profession and practice of religion involves a continual decision against the pressure of one's social environment, than there was in the world of yesterday, when it might involve nothing but social conformity. Dr Macquarrie is perhaps right in suggesting that there may be something in the history of a culture corresponding to the dark night of the soul which is a common phenomenon in the life of the individual Christian. "When we consider", he writes, "that in the history of a culture there may be ages of faith when God's reality is, it would seem, overwhelmingly and convincingly present, but also ages of secularism when God seems silent or absent, it is at least a question whether such an alternation can be entirely accounted for in terms that are immanent to the development of the culture, or whether we must suppose that at different times God may draw near or withdraw himself."[1] Fr Karl Rahner, too, may be correct when he writes:

> The apparent atrophy of the religious sense today is a passing phenomenon; in the period of vast upheaval in which we live, of which the past century of industrialism is only the beginning, it was, *in concreto*, absolutely unavoidable and to be expected.... Man's religious sense is ineradicable, nor can it, in the long run, be appeased by pseudo-objects provided by secular utopianism, economic, social or cultural.... And if this be doubted – I mean, the possibility of discerning such chances – well it is precisely for the Christian to hope against hope, knowing that God triumphs when we seem to be lost.[2]

It may be that in this present age there is no message for the Christian save that which, in Gilbert Chesterton's poem, King Alfred had to bring:

> This is the word of Mary,
>   The word of the world's desire:
> "No more of comfort shall ye get,

[1] *Principles of Christian Theology*, p. 148.
[2] *Mission and Grace*, I, pp. 53f.

> Save that the sky grows darker yet
> And the sea rises higher."[1]

These things are in the hand of God. It is our task to find, if we can, the language in which the faith can be spoken to the men and women of our time. But in doing this we must at all costs avoid the suggestion that they are in the least degree more important to God than any other men and women who have ever lived on this earth or that our century means any more to him than any other. As Mr Harry Blamires has shown in his chapter "The Tyranny of Time", the cultus of contemporaneity is the very antithesis of the Christian religion.

> We suffer [he writes] from a grossly exaggerated notion of the significance of sheer contemporaneousness. And we suffer from a correspondingly inflated estimate of the isolation of the present from the past. There is no justification, either in Christianity or reason, for the highly pressurised notion of our need at all costs to be *with* those who are living on this earth at the same time as ourselves. . . . There is no special demand upon us to agree with a person simply because he is alive. . . . The proximity of mere contemporaneousness ought surely not to weigh too heavily with the man who believes that in eternity past and present are one and that in Christ Christians of all ages are alive together.[2]

[1] *The Ballad of the White Horse*, Book iii.
[2] *A Defence of Dogmatism*, pp. 30f.

Again he writes, in words that are very pertinent to our present concern:

> The idolatry of the temporal process implicit in much recent theological thinking should now be evident. It is, of course, no accident that the pseudo-theology of men who accept an intellectual servitude to time should be accompanied by unease before the traditional formulations of the eternal/temporal relationship. The creatureliness of the human creature, the childhood status of the human creature, and the Fatherhood of God are brought into question, and fashionable talk about man growing up and becoming adult adds to that total misreading of the temporal situation which disfigures our age's thinking. A key error threading its way through recent pseudo-theology is that "time will tell". It will not. Eternity will tell.[1]

I would specially recommend this chapter, and indeed the whole of Mr Blamires's book, to any Christian who is in danger of succumbing to the *Zeitgeist*, for this is a danger that is specially seductive, and also specially lethal, in this day of the denial of God and the deification of the secular.

Beneath this servitude to the present that is characteristic of the radical theologians there lies, I believe, a fundamental rejection of the claims of reason. We might suspect this from the very terms which they use to com-

[1] ibid., p.

D

mend their doctrine: "mature", "adult", "candid", "contemporary", "relevant" and, of course, "radical" itself; but rarely does it make a simple claim to be *true*. In most of the writers this irrationalism is assumed and implicit rather than overt and professed, for most of them are by training theologians rather than philosophers, though Dr Altizer's predilection for Blake and Nietzsche is revealing. There is, however, one who is a professional philosopher, namely Dr Leslie Dewart, and in his book *The Future of Belief: Theism in a World come of age* the situation becomes perfectly clear. Not only does he take "contemporary experience" as the norm, itself exempt from criticism, by which everything, including the Christian faith, is to be judged. He rejects, under the label of "Hellenism", the notion that the truth of a belief consists in its agreement with objective reality, and he substitutes a purely subjective and fluid criterion of truth.

> Truth [he writes] is not the adequacy of our representative operations, but the adequacy of our conscious existence. . . . The nature of truth does not merely permit truth to develop, but indeed requires that it do so. For truth itself consists in a certain intensive development of man's original relation to reality given by the fact that, being a reality, he participates in being. . . . *Hence the only valid "criterion" of truth is that it create the possibility of more truth.*[1]

[1] *The Future of Belief*, pp. 92, 111 (italicisation added).

I find this last sentence quite terrifying, for it means that anything that tends to propagate its kind indefinitely is to be invested *ipso facto* with the august diadem of truth. Is not this in the last resort simply the sheer demonic glorification and deification of power? Clearly, in this view, they must upward still and onward with a vengeance who would keep abreast of truth! However, as a number of Dr Dewart's critics have pointed out, his doctrine of truth cannot even be stated without paralysing itself. To quote Dr Armand Maurer for one:

> The doctrine of the historicity of truth espoused by [Dewart's] book faces the . . . difficulty that, if it is true, it must have come into existence as a part of man's process of self-awareness and self-making, and hence it is relative to his situation in a certain moment of history. Like all truths, it must be historically relative, and not timeless and supracultural. And yet the doctrine says more than this; it pretends to be a philosophical truth valid for all times and cultures. In short, total historisation is not tenable, for the doctrine of historicity cannot be formulated without denying itself.[1]

Indeed, on its own principles, to refute this doctrine we

[1] *The Ecumenist*, V, ii (Jan-Feb. 1967), p. 25. Cf. the very detailed and piercing criticism by Bernard J. F. Lonergan, "The Dehellenisation of Dogma", in *Theological Studies*, XXVIII (June 1967), pp. 336ff.

do not need to do anything; we need only watch in silence while, like the old soldiers in the song, it simply fades away. It is only because time is precious that we need to hasten its dissolution by argument. Though they are less articulate philosophically than Dr Dewart this doctrine is, I think, common to the "radical" theologians as a group, with their disregard of the past and their obsession for being contemporary. (Dr van Buren is perhaps an exception to this generalisation, for his philosophical allegiance is to linguistic analysis, while that of the others is to various forms of existentialism.) However, there is nothing like the contemporary for becoming uncontemporary; nothing gets out of fashion so fast as the fashion, as every woman knows. The point is important, for unless we get right to the root of their epistemology we are almost certain to find ourselves at cross purposes with the radical theologians; and we shall in particular be unable to account for their puzzling inability to distinguish between our idea of God and God himself.

One of the chief difficulties which confronts us in this kind of discussion arises from the fact that the content of the word "God" may be different for the various parties to the discussion and that they may therefore, without recognising it, not be arguing about the same propositions at all. It is even more serious when the word "God" is given different contents by the same thinker in different stages of his argument, for this produces something worse than confusion, namely sheer fallacy. We can find an example of this in Dr John A. T. Robinson, who first defines "God" as the object of ultimate concern and then, subtly or inadvertently re-defining "God" in the Christian sense, argues that anyone who has an ultimate concern must, whether he knows it or not, really be a Christian.[1] (This produced, in a radio programme, a famous expostulation by Miss Marghanita Laski, who insisted that she had an ulti-mate concern but was, in fact, what would normally be called not a Christian but an atheist.) It is easy to see how the temptation arises. The less we include in our definition of God, the easier it will be to produce plausible arguments for God's existence, but the less use will the God be whose existence has been shown to be likely. On the other hand, if we include in our definition of God all that we need for the purposes of religion, the more difficult will it be to demonstrate the existence of such a being. There are thus great advantages in switching at the critical moment from one definition to the other, but, as Lord Russell once said in a somewhat similar context, they are the advantages of theft over honest toil.

The importance of distinguishing between what we might call the minimal philosophical definition of God and the theological description of God as he is under-stood in the Christian religion may, I think, be use-fully illustrated from the account given by St Thomas Aquinas in the *Summa Theologiae*; it explains the fact, which often puzzles students of the Angelic Doctor, that

[1] *Honest to God*, p. 49.

he gives his proof of the existence of God before, and not after, he tells us what God's attributes and his "proper name" are. I must, however, leave a discussion of this point to an appendix to this lecture.[1] What I have called the minimal philosophical definition of God defines God simply as the transcendent cause of the world's existence; thus the question "Does God exist?" becomes "Has the world a transcendent cause or not?" It is only after we have answered this question in the affirmative that we can go on and ask what this transcendent cause is like, for if the world does not require a transcendent cause it is obviously ridiculous to ask what kind of a transcendent cause it would require if it required one. Recognition of this distinction will, I think, acquit not only St Thomas but a good many modern writers from the charge of intellectual incoherence. I would hold that the approach developed by Dr Austin M. Farrer in his book *Finite and Infinite*[2] is in no way discredited; but it is important to recognise that the mere argument for God's existence tells us practically nothing about him unless it is supplemented by further considerations derived either from reasoning or from revelation. We must, if only as good empirical philosophers, reject any tendency to rule out natural theology on *a priori* grounds, whether that tendency comes from

[1] Cf. p. 67 infra.
[2] The argument of *Finite and Infinite*, published in 1943, has been reconsidered and strengthened by Dr Farrer in his more recent book *Faith and Speculation* (1967).

positivist philosophers or from anti-rational theologians.

I find a good example of this tendency in Dr R. Gregor Smith's book *Secular Christianity*. He first asserts, as a corollary of "the eminent historicity of faith", that "the traditional ways of 'proving' God's existence are not adequate as independent proofs. They are not adequate", he continues, "because they do not take account of the way in which faith takes its rise and its form. This is true, at least, of the cosmological, the teleological and the moral argument for the existence of God." Here we have theological apriorism in an acute form; faith demands that the existence of God cannot be demonstrated. But we are also told that "each of these arguments is able to reach the conclusion 'God exists' only because they contain the hidden pre-supposition that God exists". It is, I think, clear that Dr Gregor Smith is here using the word "God" to mean "God as he is known through the Christian revelation". To attempt to prove by reason that God defined in this way exists, would indeed be to go beyond the limits of reason, and if anyone thought he had proved it, this could only be because he had inadvertently smuggled his conclusion in, either at the beginning of his argument or during the course of it. It seems, however, that Dr Gregor Smith has himself fallen into this very confusion, otherwise he could hardly have supposed that the natural theologians whom he criticises had fallen into it when, in fact, they had not. This diagnosis is confirmed by the fact that he continues as follows:

The actual course of the arguments logically excludes this pre-supposition [sc., that God exists]. Each
of the arguments demands a leap from the con-
ditioned to the unconditioned which the discursive
reason is by its nature unable to take. Whether you
begin from the contingency of all things in the
cosmos, or from the evidences of design in nature, or
from the sovereignty of the moral will, you are
brought up short against the limits of rational
enquiry; if you begin from this world you cannot
go beyond it. Thus the logical consequence of an
enquiry into the nature of the cosmos, or of
the moral demand, is pantheism, or humanism, or
nihilism.[1]

Now I am not concerned here with the argument from
design, the "enquiry into the nature of the cosmos";
this inevitably has to face the challenge of the problem
of evil, about which I shall say something later on. Nor
am I concerned here with the argument from the moral
will, though Mr Huw Parri Owen seems to me to have
shown in his book *The Moral Argument for Christian
Theism* that the argument is not as disreputable as is
frequently assumed. What I am concerned with is the
argument from the contingency of the cosmos, which Dr
Gregor Smith, having mentioned it in the penultimate
sentence of the passage which I have just quoted, oddly
omits in the final one. His key assertion, "If you begin

[1] *Secular Christianity*, p. 59.

from this world you cannot go beyond it", is sheer dogma, and, I would maintain, very implausible dogma at that. It rules out of court without examination such not inconsiderable figures as St Augustine, St Bonaventure and St Thomas Aquinas, to say nothing of more recent figures such as William Temple, A. E. Taylor and many other Gifford Lecturers. It might appear more reasonable to suppose that if you begin from this world you *must* go beyond it, if you are to get anywhere at all. Certainly none of the alternatives offered is of any help.

Pantheism and humanism leave you where you were, with a purely contingent reality. What "nihilism" means in this context is obscure, though it suggests the position held by one of Chekhov's characters in his periods of intoxication, that "perhaps we don't really exist but only think we do". The traditional arguments may indeed need restating and developing in a modern setting. It may be well for them to start from the particular being *man*, the being which each of us is, rather than from contingent being in general, though I am not sure of this. Fr Martin D'Arcy has suggested that the argument from religious experience may well turn out to be "nothing but the old argument from contingency looked at from inside instead of from outside".[1] In any case it seems somewhat cavalier to ignore without discussion contemporary writers of the stature of Dr Austin Farrer, Dr Hywel D. Lewis and Dr Ian T.

[1] *The Nature of Belief*, p. 263.

Ramsey.[1] I can only reaffirm my conviction that those who are prepared to take the trouble will find that there is a great deal more substance in the traditional approach to theism than those who reject it on *a priori* grounds admit.

In what I have just said I do not intend to deny that our knowledge of God is knowledge of a very special, and indeed a unique, kind, but on the contrary to affirm this. Dr C. B. Daly has put the point very clearly as follows:

> If my empirical knowledge forces me to ask questions which *cannot* be answered in empirical terms, then I know that empirical knowledge is not adequate to the reality which I am. But to know that knowledge is inadequate is a valid and a most important kind of knowledge. It is a perpetual invitation to deeper reflection; but also an awareness that reflection will never come to an end of what there is to know. . . .

And again:

> Metaphysics begins with the recognition that there is mystery in being and in experience. But it is not merely the recognition of mystery. Metaphysics cannot end until it has rendered such reason of that mystery that it shall not become instead absurdity. The true alternative is not mystery *or* clarity, but mystery *or* absurdity.[2]

[1] A. M. Farrer, *Finite and Infinite, Faith and Speculation*; H. D. Lewis, *Our Experience of God;* I. T. Ramsey, *Religious Language, Models and Mystery, Christian Discourse*.

[2] "Metaphysics and the Limits of Language", in *Prospect for Metaphysics*, ed. I. T. Ramsey, pp. 199, 204.

Dr D. Z. Phillips writes to a similar effect:

> Coming to see that there is a God is not like coming
> to see that an additional being exists. If it were, there
> would be an extension of one's knowledge of facts,
> but no extension of one's understanding. Coming to
> see that there is a God involves seeing a new meaning
> in one's life, and being given a new understanding. . . .
> Discovering that there is a God is not like establish-
> ing that something is the case within a universe of
> discourse with which we are already familiar. On the
> contrary, it is to discover that there *is* a universe of
> discourse we had been unaware of.[1]

To this we might add Dr H. D. Lewis's reminder: "The
infinite is not an extension of the finite but its condition",[2] and these words of Mr Michael Novak:
"[God] is the one who makes inquiry itself intelligible.
. . . He is not an explanation among explanations, but
the explanation of why there are explanations,"[3]

All this I believe to be true but it will not take us very
far if what we are seeking is a point of entry for Christian
theism into the secularised mind of modern man. The
God of natural theology, of whom we know only that he
is the transcendent cause of the finite world and has

[1]"Faith, Scepticism and Religious Understanding", in *Religion
and Understanding*, ed. D. Z. Phillips, pp. 68, 69.

[2]*Freedom and History*, p. 282.

[3]*Belief and Unbelief*, p. 125.

whatever attributes necessarily follow from this, is at best a bleak and austere deity until natural theology is quickened and warmed by revelation. Furthermore a certain cast and attitude of mind is needed to respond to the appeal of natural theology. Even in the thirteenth century St Thomas had to admit that neither the young, the busy nor the unintelligent were likely to react positively to its unassisted advances;[1] and the necessary cast of mind would seem to be less common today than it was then. In any case, human beings differ from one another so widely in their temperaments and attainments that it is impossible to lay down one uniform guaranteed line of approach to the modern man, who is as much of an abstraction as the average British family, which, statisticians tell us, consists of one husband, one wife and slightly more than two children. In all probability, not one but a number of approaches need to be developed if Christian theism is to display its relevance and attractiveness to the wide variety of persons who together make up the human race today. This is the task primarily of the apologist and I cannot attempt to go into it in detail here. I would, however, suggest that the most hopeful starting-point will probably be found in some aspect or another of the insufficiency of the finite world.

The insufficiency of the finite world and its incapacity to satisfy either the intellect or the appetites of man has been the theme of a great deal of the most

[1] *Contra Gent*, I, iv; *S. Theol.*, II II, ii, 4c.

persistently honest literature of the present century. Franz Kafka's unfinished novels *The Castle* and *The Trial* are striking examples of this, the former with its picture of man seeking to find a place in the world but never being quite sure that there is a place for him, the latter with its picture of man as under the shadow of a judgment whose nature and authority never make themselves plain. Another example is provided by Jean-Paul Sartre's novel *La Nausée*, in which the principal character Antoine Roquentin is provoked to a disgust amounting to physical nausea by the sheer absurdity and superfluity, the ultimate pointlessness, of the black, knotty root of a chestnut-tree which obstinately goes on existing in spite of the fact that there is neither rhyme nor reason for it. These are some of the most notable instances of the expression in literary form of the conviction that neither human life nor the world of which man is a part makes any sense of itself. Neither carries within itself anything that can answer the questions or satisfy the appetites that its existence provokes. A more sensational example is provided by the contemporary novelists and dramatists of the "school of the absurd", such as Samuel Beckett, Eugène Ionesco, Harold Pinter and Edward Albee, who express their conviction of the absurdity of existence by making it even more absurd than it appears. The significant feature in this is that all these writers are atheists. I do not suggest that this provides more than a starting-point for apologetics, for it does not follow, from the fact that a world interpreted without reference to God is absurd, that a world interpreted with reference to God will be perfectly intelligible and comfortable; the world might conceivably be absurd in either case, with an absolutely incurable absurdity. Nevertheless I think there is more hope for theism when it is recognised that a world interpreted without reference to God is absurd than when it is claimed that a world interpreted without reference to God makes perfectly good sense. Man's extremity, the proverb reminds us, is God's opportunity, and so it may be here. I have just quoted Fr D'Arcy's remark that the argument from religious experience may well turn out to be nothing but the old argument from contingency looked at from inside instead of from outside: we may now perhaps add that the argument that existence is ultimately absurd may be what the old argument from contingency becomes if one is determined to reject the only interpretation of existence which removes the appearance of absurdity. The recognition of this may do something to destroy the sense of helplessness and irrelevance which so often menaces the believer today, and may enable him to re-examine the case for a theistic interpretation of life without feeling foredoomed to failure. This is not the place for that re-examination, but I cannot end this lecture without some reference to what is for many people the chief obstacle to belief, namely the problem of evil.

Few thoughtful people today would feel justified in

dismissing the problem with the simple assurance of Alexander Pope that

> . . . the first Almighty Cause
> Acts not by partial, but by gen'ral laws; . . .
> If plagues or earthquakes break not Heaven's design,
> Why then a Borgia, or a Cataline? . . .
> Why charge we Heaven in those, in these acquit?
> In both, to reason right is to submit.[1]

The ways of God are not to be vindicated to Man quite as easily as this, and in recent years the problem has forced itself on human minds more urgently than ever before. At least one distinguished Jewish thinker found himself unable, after the massacre of the Jews under Hitler, to believe any more in a God who had concern for his people. The agony with which a Christian of Jewish race was able both to retain and to deepen his faith is movingly depicted in the book significantly entitled *Theology of Auschwitz* by my friend and colleague Dr Ulrich E. Simon. However, for many the real problem is posed not so much by the quantitative aspect of human suffering – after all, one man can only suffer one man's sufferings – but by the intensity with which it can fall on one helpless individual. The classical example of this is, of course, that of Ivan in Dostoyevsky's novel *The Brothers Karamazov*, for whom the sufferings of a child of five, shut up by her parents all night in a filthy and freezing closet was by itself sufficient to

[1] *Essay on Man*, Epistle I, v.

make belief in God impossible.[1] More recently the dialogue between Fr Paneloux and the atheist Dr Rieux in Albert Camus' novel *The Plague* has posed the same problem; here again the sufferer is a young child, though the suffering is inflicted not by cruel parents but by bubonic plague.[2] Dr William Hamilton has drawn attention to a similar and very revealing passage in Joseph Heller's novel of absurdity *Catch 22*.[3] The revealing feature here is that, while rejecting belief in God, the characters in the story find themselves compelled to postulate his existence in order to have an adequate object for their moral indignation.

"What the hell are you getting so upset about?" he asked her bewilderedly in a tone of contrite amusement. "I thought you didn't believe in God."

"I don't", she sobbed, bursting violently into tears. "But the God I don't believe in is a good God, a just God, a merciful God. He's not the mean and stupid God you make him out to be."

Yossarian laughed and turned her arms loose. "Let's have a little more religious freedom between us", he proposed obligingly. "You don't believe in the God you want to, and I won't believe in the God I want to. Is that a deal?"

[1] F. Dostoyevsky, *The Brothers Karamazov*, Book V, ch. v.

[2] A. Camus, *Le Peste*, Part IV, ch. iii, cit. W. Hamilton, *The New Essence of Christianity*, pp. 47ff.

[3] J. Heller, *Catch 22*, pp. 183–5, cit. W. Hamilton, "A Note on Radical Theology", *Concilium*, IX, iii (Nov. 1967), pp. 40f.

One might be tempted to see in this passage simply an example in support of the point made earlier in this lecture, that before discussing whether God exists it is important to be agreed on the precise meaning to be given to the word "God". There is, however, more to it than this. We are confronted with a remarkable and paradoxical feature of the problem of evil as it presents itself in real life. The existential question, as distinct from the purely academic one, occurs only for the believer: "How", he agonisingly asks himself, "can a good and omnipotent God allow these things to happen?" For the unbeliever there can only be the academic question, "What is the basic character of a world in which such things occur?" He may be puzzled and even frightened, but he has no rational ground for resentment; in a godless world there is no reason why anything whatever should not occur, there is no reason why such a world should not be ultimately hideous, and if it is there is no one who can be blamed. Behind the problem itself there lies another problem: if there is no God, why should unbelievers feel there is a problem at all, for many of them certainly do? The point was expressed pungently in one of Ingmar Bergman's films: "If one can believe in God, there is no problem; if one cannot, there is no solution."[1] To which we might add: "If one cannot, why is there a problem?"

We are, it must be stressed, concerned with some-

[1]Cit. G. D. Phillips, "Through a Glass Darkly", *Clergy Review* LII (Oct. 1967), p. 802.

E

thing much more than simply deciding whether, in the world's history as a whole, there is more good than evil; as if we could first add all the goods together, then add all the evils together and finally observe which of the sums was the greater. One item of unnecessary and un-redeemed evil will leave the problem unresolved, how-ever much good there may be; this was the heart of Ivan Karamazov's atheism. In the last resort, I believe, a theist is bound to hold with St Augustine, that God would never allow evil to occur unless he was able to bring greater good out of it. But is important to see what this involves.

It involves that all the evil that there has ever been will ultimately be seen to matter no more. This is totally different from saying that it will ultimately be seen not to have mattered; and in the difference be-tween these two statements there lies hidden the whole mystery of time, as not merely a mathematical para-meter but a lived-through reality. When the evil occurred, it mattered indeed; in the end it will matter no longer. If we find it difficult to believe this in the face of the horrors of Auschwitz, the reason is, I suggest, that we find it difficult to recognise that God can do anything which very greatly exceeds what we can do ourselves. No one is likely to lose his faith in the good-ness and omnipotence of God because of five minutes' toothache; even *we* could cope with that, we feel. But Auschwitz – that would be too much even for God; even God himself could not make that no longer matter. But it is, I maintain, by affirming that God *can* do this, and by meditating upon it, that we may come to form some faint concept of what God's omnipotence really means. And in this none of the limited Gods of the various contemporary pseudo-theisms will be of any use at all. If in arguing in this way I may seem to be juggling with philosophical sophistries, I would only add that all that I have said is contained in one luminous saying of Jesus himself: "A woman when she is in travail has sorrow because her hour is come, but as soon as she is delivered of the child she remembers no more the anguish, for joy that a man is born into the world."[1] And the Apostle reminds us that "the whole creation groans and travails in pain together until now"[2].

I have said that the problem of evil is an existential and not a merely academic one, and for this reason we may find that some of the most profound insights bearing upon it are expressed through the medium of poetry rather than of theological or philosophical prose. Time will permit of only two brief references here. The first is to Gerard Manley Hopkins's poem *The Wreck of the Deutschland*, of which Philip M. Martin has written that it "is not only about the shipwreck; it is also about Christ's Passion; and yet, not so much about his Passion as about the triumph which was inherent in his Passion and was made manifest after it. It concerns the mystery of the incarnation of God, the redemptive action and the active love of God, it con-

[1] John xvi. 21. [2] Rom. viii. 22.

cerns 'the Passion and redemption working themselves out in the lives of men'".[1] I most warmly commend Canon Martin's splendid interpretative commentary on Hopkins's poem in his little book *Mastery and Mercy*. The other poem is of a very different type; it is the late fourteenth-century elegy *Pearl*, which, in a modern version by Mr Brian Stone, is included in the Penguin Classics volume *Medieval English Verse*. In it the poet is lamenting the death of his little two-year-old daughter after whom the poem is named, when she appears to him in the form of a beautiful maiden, robed and crowned in such splendour as might seem appropriate only to the Blessed Virgin Mary herself. I shall not attempt to reproduce the exquisite language of the hundred-and-one stanzas which make up the poem, but only to indicate in modern idiom the points which are relevant to our present concern. To the poet's question whether the Mother of God might not justly resent the bestowal of such glory on the humble person of poor little Pearl, the answer is given, "Mary's Son has indeed transformed me beyond all expectation, but even so my glory is as nothing compared with hers. And in any case, where I am now we have more important things to do than waste our time in jealousy; and Mary, who is the Queen of Courtesy is concerned with it least of us all." And when the poet protests that, even so, it is somewhat excessive that a two-year-old child should be given the dignity of royalty straight away, he is in-

[1] *Mastery and Mercy*, pp. 28f.

formed that there are simply no limits to the power and bounty of God.

And here we must leave the question of God for the time being. I will only stress in concluding that there can be no greater error than to suppose that we can liberate man by eliminating God. It is not because they have had too exalted an idea of God that Christians have so many crimes and failures to answer for; it is because their idea of God has been too limited and low.

"Few modern writers", Rabbi Rubenstein tells us, "have celebrated the satisfactions of the flesh and of this world so fully as Camus in his marvellous essay 'Summer in Algiers', yet this very essay describes with uncompromising clarity how those who live by the flesh have nothing but the flesh in the end. Death in Algiers was devoid of all consolation. For Camus the invincible summer was inevitably followed by the cold of autumn and winter. Of all the evils let loose from Pandora's box, Camus tells us, the worst was hope."[1] And yet we may perhaps let Camus speak the last word for us: "God is denied in the name of justice; but can the idea of justice be understood without the idea of God?"[2]

[1] *The Secular City Debate*, ed. D. Callahan, pp. 140f.
[2] Cit. by C. C. West, *The Secular City Debate*, p. 61.

APPENDIX TO CHAPTER II

In article 3 of Question ii of the *Pars Prima* St Thomas expounds the famous "Five Ways" of demonstrating that there is a God; then in the following nine questions he argues that God is simple, perfect, good, infinite, unchangeable, eternal and one. This raises the question of the definition of God that St Thomas assumed when he argued for God's existence, for clearly these attributes could not have been explicit in that definition. He had indeed mentioned in article 1 of Question ii St Anselm's definition of God as "that than which no greater can be meant", though with the substitution of *significari* for Anselm's *cogitari*. However, this was in the course of refuting Anselm's ontological argument, and he explicitly says that "we do not know what God is" (*nos non scimus de Deo quid est*). Again he writes: "We cannot know what God is, but only what he is not" (*De Deo scire non possumus quid sit, sed quid non sit*).[1] Are we then to suppose that St Thomas himself tried to prove that God exists without giving any content to the word "God"? This would seem unlikely, to say the least, and if we examine his text carefully we shall see that he was not as naïve as that.

All his Five Ways are arguments from effect to cause, in different orders of causality. He writes as follows:

When we argue from effect to cause, the effect will

[1] *S. Th.* I, iii, prol.

take the place of a definition of the cause in the proof that the cause exists; and this especially when it is God who is concerned. For when proving anything to exist we have to take as a link not what the thing is (*quod quid est*), for that question comes *after* the question whether it exists, but what its name means (*quid significet nomen*). For the names of God are derived from his effects, as we shall see, and so, when demonstrating from his effects that God exists we can take as a link what the word "God" means.[1]

It is clear from this that when St Thomas says that the effect takes the place of a definition of the cause he means that, as a preliminary definition of God, a definition sufficient simply to identify the being of which we are speaking and to distinguish it from all other possible or actual beings, we can take the formula:

God = Df the transcendent cause of the world and of the beings composing it.

Thus the question "Does God exist?" simply becomes "Have the world and its components a transcendent cause or not?" It is only after we have answered this question in the affirmative that we can go on and ask what this cause is like, for if the world does not require a transcendent cause it is obviously ridiculous to ask what kind of a transcendent cause it would require if it re-

[1] ib. ii, 2 ad 2.

quired one. And when St Thomas, having demonstrated God's existence, proceeds to argue that God is simple, perfect, good, infinite, unchangeable and one, he is still considering "how God does not exist rather than how he does" (*non . . . . quomodo sit sed potius quomodo non sit*).[1] And in all the succeeding articles about "what God is not" the recurrent question is simply what is involved in God as transcendent cause of the world; we may be surprised at the amount that St Thomas derives from this, but there is no doubt as to what he believes himself to be doing. When later on he raises the question as to how talk about God is possible, this is still true: "The names we give to God signify him in the way in which our intellect knows him. And since our intellect knows God from his creatures, it knows him as they represent him."[2]

We can now throw light upon a problem which has always embarrassed Thomist commentators, arising from the apparently casual manner in which St Thomas ends each of the Five Ways with a remark such as "We all call this God."[3] What grounds can there be for supposing that, when we have proved the existence of a first efficient cause or an absolutely necessary being, we have proved the existence of "the God and Father of our Lord Jesus Christ", the God in whom Christians believe? Very little. "We all call this God", because at this stage of the argument "God" simply corresponds to the preliminary definition, which we adopted not in

[1] ib., I, iii, prol.   [2] ib., I, xiii, 2c.   [3] ib., I, ii, 3c.

order to say everything that, as Christians, we believe about God, but simply in order to give ourselves a unique and unambiguously defined referend for the word "God". There are very real methodological advantages in following this course. It enables us to separate the argument for God's existence from discussion about what God is like and whether the Christian concept of God is self-consistent. It does not, of course, give us an irrefutable answer to the modern agnostic or atheist's rejection of any arguments for the existence of God, but it does enable us to keep distinct two questions which are often confused with each other. It enables St Thomas to talk intelligibly and intelligently about God long before he has enquired what is God's most appropriate name, and it resolves the paradox that, according to him, God's most appropriate name is not in fact "God" but "He who is".[1] This, of course, does not settle the question whether one can by pure reason deduce all the attributes of God which St Thomas claims to deduce immediately after his demonstration that God exists.

[1] S. Theol., I, xiii, 11. In my book *Existence and Analogy* (pp. 76ff), published in 1949, I took a slightly different view from that expounded above.

CHAPTER THREE

The Question of Man

I SUGGESTED IN THE LAST LECTURE THAT ONE possible point of entry for Christian theism into the secularised mind of modern man might be found in the works of such sensitive atheist novelists and playwrights as Kafka, Sartre, Camus and the contemporary school of the "absurd", with their keen perception of the insufficiency and incapacity of the finite world to satisfy either the intellect or the appetites of human beings, "the plight", as another writer has described it, "of every man in a world which is neither of his making nor of his choosing."[1] I added that this could only be a starting-point, since it does not follow, from the fact that the world does not make sense without God, that it will make sense with him; it might conceivably be incurably senseless. It is nevertheless relevant to remark that many intelligent people who have passed from unbelief to Christianity have verified in their own experience that meaninglessness has given place to meaning; Gilbert Keith Chesterton, Thomas Sterns Eliot and Jacques Maritain may be mentioned as instances that immediately occur to the mind. And there are of course multitudes of intelligent people who, having been

[1] Germaine Greer, reviewing John Grillo's play *Hello-Goodbye Sebastian* in the Cambridge Review of 29 May 1965.

brought up as Christians, have progressively experienced the power of the Christian faith to make life meaningful and who therefore have never strayed into the waste land of unbelief at all.

In the present lecture we are not concerned directly with either theistic or Christian apologetics, but with the attitude which the theology of the immediate future should adopt to the question of man; and we must begin by recognising the fact, whether we like it or not, that the writers of the school of the "absurd" represent only a minor, although an important, element in the world of the present day. The Church is faced with two other movements, of immense prestige and power, which claim to give meaning to human life and to satisfy human needs on a purely secular basis. One of these is scientific humanism; the other is Marxism.

It will be well to recognise at the start that a great deal of the plausibility with which these movements invest their pronouncements arises from a quasi-metaphysical assumption which, on their own principles, they would be very hard put to justify. Both of them, while holding that individual men and women cease to exist when they die, are accustomed to speak in glowing terms of the glorious future awaiting an entity designated by the word "Man". Man in the past was miserable and frustrated, either because of his lack of understanding of the forces of nature or because of his exploitation by priests, kings and capitalists. Man today, at least in the more enlightened regions of the earth, is very much happier than he was; and at some future date, "when science has discovered something more" or when socialisation according to Marxist principles has completed its task, man will be enjoying a condition of virtually unbounded happiness, with all his needs, both material and cultural, satisfied by the good things of this life. What must be recognised quite clearly is that on secularist principles, whether those of scientific humanism or of Marxism, the word "man" used in these several contexts does not designate the same being; to use the language of the logicians, we have an example of the fallacy of equivocation. The man who was miserable in the past is not the man who is better off today, and neither of these is the man who will be so happy in the future, since each of these men ceases to exist when he dies. The story of Man making his triumphal progress through the ages is a sheer myth; like Sarah Gamp's friend Mrs Harris, "there's no sich person".

It is important to get this point quite clear. I am not denying that secularists frequently perform acts of great and admirable self-denial for the sake of their children or grandchildren or even for the sake of persons in distant lands as yet unborn, and that they do not perform these acts simply for the personal pleasure and satisfaction which they derive from them; that is not the point at issue. The point is that the story which they commonly tell in order to make sense of their behaviour – the story about "Man" suffering in one age and rejoicing in another – is directly contrary to the belief which they explicitly hold about *men*. If one holds that human beings survive death, it is possible to make some sense of the story, even if a somewhat metaphorical interpretation has to be given it. There is not, indeed, one identical inhabitant of this planet who is the hero of all the episodes, but there is one growing society of human beings, each of whom goes on existing indefinitely after his first appearance and will share with the rest of the human race in its final condition: "man", in the sense of "mankind", is a growing, and ultimately simultaneous, social organism. There is no such unity of mankind on the secularist doctrine; for it, mankind consists of an aggregate of certain individual human beings at one time and of an aggregate of entirely different individual human beings two centuries later. There might be a way out from this conclusion if one held a quasi-Platonic view that there is one altogether real and transcendent Idea of Man, which acquires imperfect and temporary instantiation in individual human beings, and that it is this transcendent Idea which, in its various instances, is the hero of the human epic; but such a view would certainly not be congenial to the typical scientific humanist, and, while it might seem to have Hegelian echoes in the dialectical aspects of dialectical materialism, it would certainly not appeal to the materialist aspects. Nor would the secularist derive any comfort from the theological doctrine that, in a very real though analogical sense, all men are one man in Adam and in Christ; that would appear to him to be sheer myth. It would, however, on his own principles, be no more of a myth than is his own story of the adventure of Man through the ages. And this can hardly be too strongly stressed, because it is this hypostatisation of Man, in defiance of the secularist doctrine about men, that lends most of its attractiveness to the picture of human history which official secularism puts forward. One of the most notable examples of this is provided by Dr C. H. Waddington's able and interesting book *The Ethical Animal*, which makes as good a case as any for the outlook of scientific humanism but becomes intellectually incoherent at just this point.

Here it may be well to interject that in describing a particular view as secularist no suggestion is intended that on such a view man's welfare consists in purely material satisfactions. A secularist is not necessarily given to the pursuit of the grosser pleasures of food, drink and sex. He may be a highly cultured person, absorbed in the pursuit of philosophy, art or science, or in the promotion of the welfare of men and women less fortunately placed than himself. What makes him a secularist is his conviction that there is no life other than "this life", and no world other than "this world". As Dr Demant has written:

The essential characteristic of secularism is independent of the nature which secularism gives to what it regards as ultimately real; it is still secularist even when that reality is mental or spiritual, and not only when it is material or biological. . . .

The secularisms of today have this in common, *that they hold the meaning of the world to lie within itself.*[1]

I have said that secularism is able to make sense of its story of human progress only by hypostatising Man in a way that is inconsistent with its basic belief about men. I must now add that, even if this difficulty can be overcome, secularism, at least in the form of scientific humanism, cannot find any convincing argument for supposing that the human race has the kind of future which it predicts. From the purely scientific point of view, there is no reason to suppose that man has any future at all. He has nothing to rely on except his own wits, and in spite of his great scientific and technological achievements, his capacity to solve the problems which he has created for himself is by no means self-evident. The two great menaces which confront him today, those of the population explosion and of nuclear, chemical and biological warfare, may well destroy him, and, if he finds his way through those, his ultimate fate as a tiny speck in a vast universe is highly problematical. The optimism about man's future which is typical of most scientific humanists might be justified if they believed in a personal Providence which had a special concern for man, but it is totally unjustified on a

[1] *Religion and the Decline of Capitalism*, pp. 113, 111 (italicisation added).

secularist view. Some, indeed, of the more thoughtful secularists have recognised this. Lord Russell's famous essay "A Free Man's Worship", which depicted man as standing, with his head bloody but unbowed, in a Henleyesque defiance of a ruthless universe, and H. G. Wells's transition from the optimism of *Men like Gods* to the pessimism of *The Fate of Homo Sapiens*, represent a more realistic type of secularism than that of some other writers.

Marxism calls for treatment by itself and I shall refer to it later on in this lecture. Before doing that I must make some reference to the fascinating and controversial figure of Pierre Teilhard de Chardin. As is well known, the English translation of Teilhard's most famous work, *The Phenomenon of Man*, was introduced to the public with an enthusiastic preface by his fellow-anthropologist Sir Julian Huxley, who is neither a Christian nor a believer in any kind of transcendent deity. Their common feature was a conviction that, on purely scientific grounds, the evolution of life on this planet had a kind of inbuilt urge towards the production of man, whose ancestry could be traced in a central path of development, which avoided the dead-ends of stabilisation or extinction in which all other species had found themselves. How far, in Huxley's view, this appearance of purpose could be reduced to the operation of natural selection on biological mutations is not perhaps easy to decide, but for Teilhard it was nothing less than a quasi-conscious teleological urge which ultimately succeeded in expressing itself in the fully self-conscious and intelligent species *Homo sapiens*. For both of them (and on this point Waddington would agree, if on few others) the emergence of man initiated a novel and vastly accelerated stage in the evolutionary process, since man, in virtue of his self-consciousness and his intelligence, can deliberately plan the future development of other species and also of his own. For Teilhard it was obvious that the present phase would culminate with the spread of man over the whole surface of the earth, and he often spoke of this human film or *noösphere* as if it was closely analogous to a plastic envelope. (Incidentally it may be noticed that the population explosion seems to have been for Teilhard a matter much more for satisfaction than for alarm). He viewed with little enthusiasm the possibility of man colonising other worlds than this earth; the next stage in evolution he envisaged as taking place not in a physical but in a spiritual dimension, in the concentration of human minds upon an ultimate focus which he called the "Omega-point" and in which he saw them as forming a great psychic organism without their own distinct individualities being destroyed. And all this he claimed to hold on purely scientific grounds; the further identification of the Omega-point with the formation of the Total Christ, the redeemed human race incorporated into the human nature of the incarnate Son of God, was achieved not on scientific grounds but as a consequence of the Christian revelation. It is not surprising that a vision as audacious as

F

this caused misgivings in both scientific and theological circles, though his friend and fellow-Jesuit Père Henri de Lubac seems to have successfully defended his orthodoxy,[1] which has been further vindicated by such writers as Fr Christopher Mooney.[2] The whole corpus of Teilhardian literature is immense and in some circles something like a cultus seems to have grown up. Whatever may be the final judgment of his work, on both its scientific and its theological side, this at least can now be said, that he attempted, as no one else in this century seems to have attempted, to integrate biological evolution with Christian eschatology. He saw the emergence of man within the evolutionary process and the incorporation of man into Christ as two stages in the working out of one divinely guided plan, the *anakephalaiōsis* of which the apostolic writer speaks,[3] the gathering up of all things into Christ. Although Teilhard was led to his vision from his studies as an anthropologist and palaeontologist, there is, as I have pointed out elsewhere,[4] a very close similarity between the "Christogenesis" of which he writes and the "Christification"[5] of the universe which is a constant theme of the theology of the Eastern Orthodox Church. This is all the more striking in view of

[1] *The Faith of Teilhard de Chardin; The Religion of Teilhard de Chardin.*

[2] *Teilhard de Chardin and the Mystery of Christ.*

[3] Ephesians i. 10.

[4] *The Christian Universe*, pp. 91ff.

[5] This term is used by Fr. Paul Evdokimov in his book *L'Orthodoxie*, p. 113.

the fact that Teilhard appears to have had little knowledge of, or interest in, Eastern Christendom. The further exploration of the territory which he has opened up may well be of ecumenical, as well as apologetic, importance; my own introduction to Teilhard's writings, some time before any of them had been translated into English, came from a Russian monk who had spent many years on Mount Athos, Father (now Archbishop) Basil Krivoshein. It is, I suggest, along these lines, rather than along those of the so-called "radical" theologians of the death-of-God school, that a fruitful dialogue with the contemporary world may be carried on.

Turning now to Marxism, it is hardly surprising, in view of the political situation of the last half century and the repressive attitude of the governments of most Communist countries towards all forms of religion, that dialogue has been slow in developing. Nevertheless, such dialogue is clearly envisaged by Pope Paul's encyclical *Ecclesiam Suam* and the Constitution *Gaudium et Spes* of Vatican II; I might add that for many years there has been in the Church of England a small but vigorous group of Christians of extremely left-wing sympathies and that a similar, but apparently quite independent, movement has recently appeared in English Roman Catholicism centred on the journal *Slant*. Perhaps the most useful discussion of the basic theoretical issues is to be found in the short work by the French Communist Professor Paul Garaudy, *From Anathema to*

Dialogue, which is based on a lecture given at St Michael's College, Toronto, in 1965, and to which Fr Karl Rahner and Fr J. B. Metz have respectively contributed an Introduction and an Epilogue.

In any dialogue it is, of course, essential to register both the common assumptions and the divergences of the parties involved; indeed, without some common assumptions it is impossible for dialogue to get under way. Fr Rahner sees a starting point in the notion of man as by his very essence orientated to the future. "Christianity", he writes, "is . . . the religion of becoming, of history, of self transcendence, of the future. . . . The tendency towards the absolute future has indeed its reason, its standard, an essence behind it, which casts before it a horizon of the possible, a law which is followed. But since the final reason is the absolute fulness of the reality of God and the final goal precisely this God who appoints the beginning by making himself the goal, then any conception of essence and nature is indeed truly realistic solely if it is understood in the light of the future which alone reveals the beginning."[1] In other words, man is essentially an *open* being, who can find his fulfilment only in union with God and who therefore has an inbuilt urge to this union. The basic question at issue between Christians and Marxists is thus, in Rahner's own words, "whether the Marxist expectation of the future is the direct opposite of the Christian doctrine of the absolute future

[1] op. cit., p. 13.

of the individual human being and of mankind, whether then they directly contradict one another, *or* whether the Christian doctrine of the future really only fills an empty space left inevitably by the Marxist expectation of the future, since it [sc. Marxism] aims merely at a possible, genuine, intra-mundane future of man."[1] Rahner goes on to argue that, while Christianity does not promise any intra-mundane future utopia, it has nevertheless a real concern for the genuine and appropriate earthly target and rejects only the view that man's ultimate future is anything less than union with God himself. He adds that religion "is not the solution of those questions which arise in this world . . . *between* the individual realities in their mutual relationship, but the solution of the question concerned with the *totality* of these plural realities."[2]

In the body of his book Dr Garaudy insists on the difference, as he sees it, between the old-fashioned type of materialism, for which religion was, purely and simply, a pernicious error, and the dialectical materialism of Marxism, for which religion was a praiseworthy, although a mistaken, attempt to satisfy a genuine demand of the human mind. In an eloquent and moving passage, he writes:

We perfectly understand the need, brought forth by suffering, for perfect communion and for a love so all-embracing that those who suffered never believed

[1] ib., p. 11f.   [2] ib., p. 22.

they could find it anywhere but in God. Indeed, we find it a beautiful thing that man, in his suffering, conceived such dreams, such hopes, conceived the infinite love of Christ. It is this act of faith that proves that man never considers himself wholly defeated. And thus he witnesses to his greatness. This is why we neither despise nor criticise the Christian for his faith, his love, his dreams, his hopes. Our own task is to labour and to struggle, lest they remain eternally distant or illusory. Our task as Communists is to draw near to man in his most glorious dreams and his most sublime hopes, to draw near to him in a real and practical way, so that Christians themselves might find here on our earth a beginning of their heaven.[1]

Garaudy finds an accurate statement of the issue between Communism and Christianity in the following words of an anonymous Catholic:

I [that is, the Catholic] say that, whatever happens, the man who is free and who freely chooses, without being stupefied by existence, will never be separated from God. And you [the Marxist] say that when man is no longer in need of distraction from his misery, when he no longer feels the need to escape from awful necessity by telling stories to himself, such a free and independent man will do without God. . . . The issue thus joined, I am ready to argue."[2]

[1]ib., p. 75.   [2]ib., p. 76.

"A fine challenge," comments Garaudy, "and one which must be accepted." And he goes on to argue that Marxism is not simply negative in its atheism, but "must assimilate from the rich Christian heritage . . . an interest in the questions men ask about the meaning of their life and their death, about the problem of their origin and their end, about the demands of their thought and their heart."[1] Where, as he sees it, religion is at fault is not in recognising the validity of these questions but in supposing that they can receive an answer. Furthermore, he tells us,

what is true of knowledge is also true of action: man achieves a growing mastery over nature, society and his own future, but if his power ceases to grow, he will be ever-militant and never-triumphant, if only because he comes up against the final limitation, which is death. He no more arrives at the total "beatitude" to which he aspires than he arrives at "total knowledge". Once again, religion claims to provide a metaphysical answer to this exigency. . . .

On the level of knowledge, the religions, starting from a real need, transformed into answer something which pertained to the order of question. In precisely the same fashion, on the level of action, the religions, and Christianity above all, transformed an exigency into a promise – and even into a presence: from the exigency of mediation, they passed over to the presence of a mediator.[2]

[1] ib., p. 77.   [2] ib., p. 78.

In his subsequent pages Garaudy repeatedly makes this point:

> For the Marxist, the infinite is absence and exigency, while for the Christian, it is promise and presence. . . .
>
> For a Christian, transcendence is the act of God who comes towards him and summons him. For a Marxist, it is a dimension of man's activity which goes out beyond itself towards its far-off being. . . .
>
> If we reject the very name of God, it is because the name implies a presence, a reality, whereas it is only an exigency which we live. . . . We can live this exigency, and we can act it out, but we cannot conceive it, name it or expect it. Even less can we hypostatise it under the name of transcendence. Regarding this totality, this absolute, I can say everything except: It is. For it is what is always deferred, and always growing, like man itself. . . .
>
> We are undoubtedly living, Christians and Marxists alike, the exigency of the same infinite, but yours is presence while ours is absence.[1]

It is impossible not to be impressed with both the nobility and the humility of Garaudy's exposition:

> Is it to impoverish man [he asks] to tell him that he lives as an incomplete being, that everything depends upon him, that the whole of our history and its sig-

[1] ib., pp. 80, 82, 83.

nificance is played out within man's intelligence, heart and will, and nowhere else, that we bear full responsibility for this; that we must assume the risk, every step of the way, since, for us atheists, nothing is promised and no one is waiting?

I think that Marxist atheism deprives man only of the illusion of certainty, and that the Marxist dialectic, when lived in its fulness, is ultimately richer in the infinite and more demanding still than the Christian transcedence.

To be sure, it is undoubtedly such only because it bears within itself the extraordinary Christian heritage, which it must investigate still more.[1]

In such a Communist as Professor Garaudy we have, I suggest, the exponent of an outlook which deserves to be taken with the utmost seriousness. It is, in this context, quite irrelevant to enquire whether individual Marxists or professedly Marxist governments invariably put their Marxist principles into practice, just as it is irrelevant to enquire whether individual Christians or professedly Christian governments invariably put into practice the principles of the Christian religion. There is a place for that enquiry, but it is not here. Garaudy himself distinguishes the political and historical discussion from the scientific and philosophical. But he also asserts – and here there is, no doubt, room for further exploration – that "completely human faith in our task

[1] ib., p. 83.

does not mutilate man of any of the dimensions which have been won because of faith in God, and that faith in a transcendent God never limits or curbs faith in the human task."[1] It is positions such as this with which, as I see it, the theology of the future will have to concern itself. Fr Metz, in his Epilogue to Garaudy's book, pinpoints one of the fundamental issues. He frankly admits that "particular social groupings [have been] canonised in the name of Christianity and that for the poor and oppressed comforting words about the hereafter were all too speedily available" and that "the Church made her criticism of the mighty in this world often far too softly and frequently much too late." But, he adds, the question which remains is this: "Are there really only self-alienations which – as Marxism supposes – can be overcome by social efforts and which we Christians canonise with the aid of theology of the hereafter and of original sin? Are there not rather forms of human self-alienation which cannot be dissolved by lifting them out of the economic-social situation – no matter how successfully – and from which man will always draw the 'pain of his finiteness'? Are there not self-alienations which cannot be simply reduced to the effect of a social, utopian expectation?"[2] And Metz makes this very significant point:

The value of a humanism is ultimately decided – in my opinion – by the hermeneutic and productive

[1]ib., p. 97.   [2]ib., pp. 119, 120.

power it develops for those frontier situations in human existence, those "self-alienations" for which there can be no simple and purely social solutions: for guilt, concupiscence, death. Do we really find in Marx a more instructive answer to these questions than we do in Jesus?

Nevertheless, Metz expresses gratitude to Garaudy for making one essential point, for "the development of the awareness that I, as an individual, can realise my hope only by trying to make over such a hope to others; the development of the awareness that I can realise my freedom only as concrete decision for others' freedom – against every form of enslavement of man."[1] And he criticises strongly the tendency in much modern theology of the "existential" and "demythologising" type to "make salvation a wholly private affair."[2]

The development of a constructive dialogue with Marxism would indeed appear to be one of the most urgent tasks for Christian theologians, since something like one third of the world's present population – human beings redeemed by Christ – are living under Marxist régimes. The avowed hostility of most of those régimes to all forms of religion and the assumption that Christian and Marxist doctrines are too basically incompatible for intelligible conversation to be possible between them has in the past made even the most tentative approaches few in number and hesitant in

[1] ib., p. 122. [2] ib., p. 124.

character. Nevertheless, the dialogue with Marxism is of no less importance than the dialogue with scientific humanism and the dialogue with the non-Christian religions. And quite apart from the investigation of the relation of these non-Christian systems to Christianity considered simply as systems, there is the question of equal if not greater urgency, of what God is doing through them. This question was put with special pungency as regards Hinduism by the Indian Roman Catholic priest Fr Raymond Panikkar in his book *The Unknown Christ of Hinduism*. In this work he argued that, while Christ and not Hinduism is the saviour of mankind, sincere Hindus are saved by Christ *through* Hinduism and not apart from it.[1] Clearly this assertion raises many difficult problems for theology in both the theoretical and the practical realm, but its fundamental truth would seem impossible to deny without also denying the universality of salvific grace. And if this is true about the non-Christian religions it must, *mutatis mutandis*, be true about atheism as well. Vatican II was quite explicit about this in more than one of its decrees. "Divine Providence", it declared in the Constitution on the Church, "does not deny the necessary aids to salvation to men who, through no fault of their own, have not yet reached an express acknowledgment of God, yet strive with the help of divine grace to attain an upright life."[2] The point is simply this: since men are saved by Christ, wherever men are saved Christ is at work; and,

[1] op. cit., p. 54.   [2] *Lumen Gentium*, n. 16.

because men are not isolated individuals but are organically integrated into the life of the communities to which they belong, if they are saved in those communities Christ must be at work in those communities too. The inter-relation of the individual and the corporate aspects of human beings are, of course, intricate, delicate and mysterious, and neither must be so stressed as to eliminate the other, but it is surely impossible for any theology which holds that grace perfects nature without destroying it, to admit that, as regards his salvation, a man is approached by God solely in his character as an individual, the social aspect of his nature being entirely excluded. Were this the case, man would not be saved in the totality of his being, *quod maxime absurdum videtur*. This is no novel hypothesis, for there has been a persistent, if sometimes underemphasised, strain in Christian thought which has maintained that, by the very fact of becoming man, the Son of God brought about a change in the whole human race and in human nature as such, a genuine initiation of the renewal of humanity itself. The translation in the Anglican Prayer Books of one luminous verse of the *Te Deum* distorts the downright realism of the Latin original. *Tu ad liberandum suscepturus hominem non horruisti Virginis uterum*: not "When thou tookest upon *thyself to deliver man* . . ." but "When thou tookest upon thyself *man to deliver him*, thou didst not disdain a Virgin's womb." I do not think we shall ever achieve a satisfactory theology of either the Fall, original sin or redemption unless we discard the nominalist tendency to look upon human beings as simply isolated individuals, and recover the sense of both sin and salvation as having not only an individual aspect – they certainly have that – but a corporate aspect as well. Indeed two of the basic truths about man which the theology of the future will need to develop and to interpret in the concrete setting of the modern world are, first, that human beings are essentially open towards God and, secondly, that they are essentially open to one another. Only by keeping these two truths in equipoise can we hope to avoid, on the one hand, the totalitarianism, whether overt or concealed, which treats men as merely interchangeable and discardable units in a gigantic social machine, and, on the other hand, the excessive individualism which leads men either to seal themselves off in private worlds of their own or else, in an attitude of banditry, to prey upon their fellows and exploit them for their own selfish ends.

There are indeed many aspects of the Christian teaching about man which need to be profoundly explored and extensively developed in the context of the needs and aspirations of the present day if the Church is to perform the tasks and seize the opportunities with which God confronts it in the modern world. The doctrine that a human being is not just a soul temporarily inhabiting and utilising an animal body but is a genuine twofold unity, consisting of a spiritual and a material part interwoven and interacting in a most mysterious and intimate way, acquires enhanced relevance at a time when so many difficult ethical problems have been created by our increased knowledge of the psychological effects of sensory conditioning and drug administration and by our growing ability to manipulate human genetic material and the process of procreation. In such a setting no relevant word can be spoken either by the angelism which identifies a man with his soul or by the existentialism which limits each man's concern to his immediate confrontation by his own consciousness. It appears that for the first time the Church is being forced to take really seriously the doctrine of the psychophysical composition of man and to explore its content and its implications. We have already seen the importance of recognising a further duality-in-unity in man, namely that of his individual and corporate aspects. And, in connection especially with Teilhard de Chardin, we have seen the necessity of an understanding of God's providential government of the universe which draws together both man's emergence from the evolutionary biological process and also his destiny in the body of Christ and the vision of God. Here there is almost limitless scope for the theology and the theologians of the future.

In concluding this lecture I shall mention briefly only two of the many other aspects of the doctrine of man which are of special interest at the present day. The first is that of the unity of the human race.

There does not seem to be any clear agreement among anthropologists and palaeontologists on the two questions of monophylism and monogenism, that is to say, whether all the existing human groupings are descended from one common anthropoid stock and, if so, whether they are all descended from one pair of human ancestors. I think, however, that most of them would answer the first question in the affirmative and the second in the negative, for it is the general opinion that new species arise rather from a change in the distribution of genetic characters (including those due to new mutations) in a group than through descent from one particular individual in whom some new character has appeared. Pope Pius XII, it will be recalled, in the encyclical *Humani Generis* ruled out the polygenist view on the ground that, unless the whole human race was descended from a single human pair, it was difficult to see how the doctrine of original sin could be maintained. Since 1950, however, theologians have tended to understand both the Fall and redemption in a much more corporate sense and this has led to an understanding of original sin which does not seem necessarily to demand the monogenist view.[1] What is necessary to Christian faith is what we may call the "theological unity" of the human race, that is to say, such a participation in a common nature that the assumption of human nature by the divine Word has renewed the whole human race

[1] Cf., e.g., Bruno Webb, "The Species Adam", *Downside Review*, LXXXV (1967), pp. 295ff; *Concilium*, VI, iii (June 1967), symposium on Evolution; K. Rahner, *Theological Investigations*, I, pp. 230ff; R. J. Pendergast, *Downside Review*, LXXXII (1964), pp. 189ff.

and his death and resurrection has redeemed it. Whether, and in what sense, the human race forms one species from the biological point of view is not unimportant but is, theologically speaking, a secondary question. The eminent zoologist Sir Alister Hardy was emphatic that "the species is something which is not just a matter of judgment but has a quite definite *objective reality*."[1] The chief ground for this assertion is the fact that, while all branches of the human race appear to be able to interbreed, it does not seem possible for human beings to interbreed with any other animals. This is of much more importance for the secularist humanist, since for him the idea of a theological unity of mankind is absurd and the only unity which he can conceive is one based on scientific evidence. Even so, it is not altogether clear that a unity of mankind based simply on the possibility of interbreeding implies that universality of basic human rights which, to their credit, most secularists are anxious to defend. We have in fact a somewhat paradoxical situation. Christians, by their belief that all men are made by God in his image and have been redeemed by the death and resurrection of Christ, are committed to maintaining the basic value and dignity of all men, but so little have they acted on the consequences of their belief that the history of the professedly Christian nations has been blackened by the slave-trade, colonialism and economic exploitation. On

[1] *The Living Stream*, p. 96. Hardy held that this was true about species in general and not only about man.

G

the other hand, many secularist humanists have shown a concern for the welfare of men simply as men that, on the grounds of their own theories, they would find it difficult to defend. Clearly there is room here for dialogue between Christians and secularists, but there is also need for a purely theological reinvestigation of the nature of human unity in the light of scientific research into the origin and past history of man.

The last question on which I shall touch is that of death, which shares with birth the characteristic of being the most universal experience of mankind. In spite of its universality – or perhaps because of this – it is remarkable how many contemporary discussions of man pay little or no attention to it. We have already noticed the way in which scientific humanists tend to gloss over the fact that individual men die by conferring a spurious immortality upon a fictitious entity called Man. It is more surprising that a recent book of essays on the Christian understanding of man, which put up a powerful defence for belief in God against the more extreme "radical" theologians, contained only one reference to the fact that men die;[1] as far as the rest of the book was concerned we might all of us be immortal. The brilliant young Jesuit theologian Robert L. Richard, who was himself taken from us by death at an early age, remarked on a similar omission in the writings of Paul van Buren, John A. T. Robinson and Harvey Cox.

[1] William Nicholls (ed.), *Conflicting Images of Man*.

> The Robinson-Cox secularisation [he wrote] is without a theology of death. It is a very excellent thing to insist, as both do, that the Christian must not live in the world as though he really lived elsewhere all the time. But it is a very mistaken thing to give the impression, as both seem to do, that the Christian must live in this world as though he were to live here for ever. . . . To be sure, both Robinson and Cox believe in an afterlife. . . . But in neither of the two authors is the affirmation of immortality, or better of the specifically Christian resurrection from the dead, a truly operative religious or theological principle.[1]

I do not myself see how we can dispense with the traditional Christian doctrine that the human soul is separated from the body at death and will be reunited with it at the general resurrection, but I think this has often been understood in a very superficial way. I am not thinking merely about the problem of the identity of the resurrection body, a problem which is intractable only if one adheres to a view of matter which science has for some time now abandoned. I am thinking rather of the way in which death has been thought of as a purely passive process, something which simply *happens* to a man and releases his soul to meet its Creator. What has often been lacking is the recognition that dying is an act which the dying person *performs*, an all-inclusive and self-committing act. This insight has been given fresh

[1] *Secularisation Theology*, p. 169.

expression by Fr Ladislaus Boros in two original and impressive small books *The Moment of Truth* and *Pain and Providence*. He asserts that "in death the soul is confronted with the totality of its subjective dynamism of being (death as total self-encounter), by entering completely into the pancosmic world-relationship, into the basis of the world (death as total presence to the world)." "If", he argues, "the being that is man reaches the climax of his adulthood only in death, we can understand why it is in death that Christ's humanity became the perfect instrumental cause of our redemption, and why it is in death that it effected that full self-surrender to the Father, that reconciled us with God." "When Christ's human reality was planted, in death, right at the heart of the world, within the deepest stratum of the universe, the stratum that unites at root bottom all that the world is, at that moment in his bodily humanity he became the real ontological ground of a new universal scheme of salvation embracing the whole human race." "We see that at Christ's death the whole world entered upon a cosmic spring the harvest of which will be the remaking of our universe in newness and splendour at the end of time." Thus, for each one of us, death "is an encounter with Christ realised in the essential sign of the basis of the world and of the spiritual dynamism of man"; it "is man's first completely personal act, and is therefore, by reason of its very being, the centre above all others for the awakening of consciousness, for freedom, for the encounter with God, for the final decision about one's eternal destiny."[1] Fr Karl Rahner, too, has developed the suggestion that death, so far from releasing the soul from any concern with matter, brings it into a new relation to the whole of the material universe.[2] Clearly we are here in the realm of speculation, but it is better to speculate about death than to ignore it. What is at any rate certain is that we shall all have to experience it, and no discussion of the human situation is either Christian or realistic unless it takes death into account. In doing this, the theology of the future will need to pay attention to all that medical science is in the process of discovering about the purely somatic aspect of dying, but this, while it will enrich and deepen the Christian understanding of death, will certainly not supersede it. More than this we are not yet in a position to say.

I have touched only briefly in this lecture on the significance, for our understanding of man, of the fact that the Son of God has taken human nature upon himself. This will, however, fall within the theme of our next lecture, on the Question of Christ.

[1] *The Moment of Truth*, pp. 162, 144, 149, 150, 164, 165.
[2] *On the Theology of Death* (Quaestiones disputatae); *Theological Investigations*, II, pp. 203ff.

CHAPTER FOUR

The Question of Christ

IF, AS I ASSERTED IN THE SECOND OF THESE lectures, the question of God is primary in Christian theology, the question of Christ is central. Even those "radicals" who wish to eliminate God from the Christian religion can hardly wish to eliminate Christ, for if they did that how could they retain any claim to the adjective "Christian"? It is nevertheless important to enquire just what it is that is being asserted when a writer claims that his theology is Christian, for many of the imaginal and emotional associations of the word "Christ" can linger on in a system that quite clearly does not understand the word in the traditional theological sense or even in the sense in which it has commonly been understood by sincere, but untheological Christians. Thus, for example, Dr Paul van Buren, when he wrote *The Secular Meaning of the Gospel*, extolled the character and teaching of Christ in such moving terms that many of his less perceptive readers overlooked the fact that, on his own view, this person Christ to whom he was so deeply devoted no longer existed, since neither Christ nor anyone else could survive bodily death. The metaphor of "contagion" which van Buren used to denote the propagation of the Christian religion down the ages is itself revealing, since a physical contagion can continue to pass from one infected person to another long after the body of the person in whom the disease first declared itself has ceased to exist. But at least for van Buren it was important that Christ once existed, even if, to adapt a famous phrase of William Pitt, we could only say that Christ saved himself by his exertions and his followers by his example. One cannot say as much for such a writer as Professor Richard B. Braithwaite, who, in his celebrated Eddington Lecture of 1955 entitled *An Empiricist's View of the Nature of Religious Belief*, maintained that, while, in order to retain his title, a Christian was bound, in addition to committing himself to an agapeistically policed way of life, to entertain the "Christian stories", he was under no obligation to believe those stories or even to believe that Christ ever existed. One cannot repress a mild feeling of surprise at Professor Braithwaite's confidence in the power of great literature to influence human actions; even Pelagius himself might have wondered at the naïvety of so wholehearted a disciple. But, to compare van Buren and Braithwaite, there might seem to be little difference in practice between two thinkers who, while differing about the importance of the past existence of Christ, agree on the unimportance of his existence today.

I cannot see how any realistic doctrine of sin and salvation can be satisfied with a Saviour whose very existence at the present day is problematical. It is, I suppose, just possible that a very crude substitutionary doctrine of the atonement might hold that Christ did everything that was needed for our salvation when he died as our substitute on the Cross and that it was therefore quite irrelevant whether or not he existed now, but I am quite sure that such a belief falls far short of the normal belief of Christians about their relation to Christ, whom they would claim as their present Saviour. Neither theology nor Christian experience can be satisfied with it. And together with this emphasis upon the present existence of Christ it is important to stress his uniqueness. Indeed the two are connected, for if Christ was not unique it is conceivable that somebody other than he might do for us today what Christ did for his contemporaries and in that case Christ's present non-existence would not matter. Some great cause, God's new Messiah, might offer each the bloom or blight, and that Messiah would not need to be Jesus of Nazareth. However, even the most liberal theology that could claim any continuity with historic Christendom would feel obliged to maintain the uniqueness of Jesus as the one Saviour, the same yesterday, today and for ever. The difficulty of liberal theology is to find a ground for this claim. It can be illustrated by reference to the late J. F. Bethune-Baker.

Bethune-Baker was, of course, well known as the author of a very clear and useful book on the theology of the first four centuries which has stood in good stead two generations of theological students. He was distinguished as much for his firm adherence to the ortho-dox position in the early trinitarian and Christological controversies as for his determination not to allow that adherence to affect his own views as a twentieth-century theologian. Like many of his day he was convinced that the key to a modern Christology was to be found in the theory of evolution, though, in a way somewhat like that in which Hegel saw the dialectical process reaching its climax in the German state of his time, Bethune-Baker saw the evolutionary process as coming to its climax and term in Jesus of Nazareth. He thus asserted, in criticising the Christology of a more conservative contemporary, that "what is *ex hypothesi* potential in all men – that is the complete union of the human with the divine – was actualised in" Christ.[1] If this statement is to be taken *au pied de la lettre*, if can only mean that Jesus was one – presumably the first – of a series of men in whom the human and the divine were completely united. Whether any other of the members of the series had yet appeared might not be clear, but what is clear is that there was nothing to prevent this, and that Jesus' position was unique only in his priority in time. Indeed even that priority might seem to be doubtful, for who could deny that such a figure might have appeared centuries before Jesus in the depths of the Amazonian forests or on some remote island in the Pacific Ocean? Now I am sure that Bethune-Baker, in spite of such remarks as that just quoted, did believe that Jesus was unique and that his uniqueness was not

[1] Review of H. M. Relton, *A Study in Christology*, in *Journal of Theological Studies*, XX (1919), p. 187.

purely accidental. It is, however, equally clear that he
was unable to expound or to justify that uniqueness in
the categories of thought that he had adopted. With
the moralistic and antimetaphysical outlook that was
typical of the liberal theologians of his day, he saw no
special difficulty in the union of the divine and the
human in a particular historic individual, but such a
phrase as "*ex hypothesi* [the hypothesis being the evolutionary hypothesis, presumably] potential in all men"
shows that he could have been thinking only of the
moral union which, whether justly or unjustly, has been
attributed to Nestorius. A similar criticism holds against
the exposition of one of Bethune-Baker's disciples, Dr W.
Norman Pittenger, who virtually identifies the humanity
and the divinity of Jesus but to some extent mitigates
this identification by holding that nobody except Jesus
is fully and truly human. In Pittenger's book *The Word
Incarnate*, the absence of a clear metaphysical distinction
between the divine and the human gives the impression
that he is unable to distinguish between a Nestorian and
a Chalcedonian Christology.

It is interesting to compare Bethune-Baker's outlook
with that of a writer half a century later, namely Dr
John Knox, in his recent book *The Humanity and
Divinity of Christ*. (Incidentally, the order of the two
abstract nouns is significant.) Knox is not committed to
evolutionism as Bethune-Baker was, and he sees that it
is impossible to identify the divine with the human,
even when the human is raised to a supreme level, since

divinity implies pre-existence and humanity excludes it. And he cannot be satisfied with a purely moral union of the human with the divine in Christ. The consequence is that Knox is unable to see the development of Christology in the New Testament as anything other than an oscillation between incompatible positions, from an initial adoptionism through a kenotic phase to docetism, though, as he makes plain, docetism was not the final form of the story which the Church came to accept. Anything like a homogeneous development is ruled out, nor is Knox willing to accept the classical Chalcedonian doctrine in anything other than a highly symbolic and mythological interpretation. For him the personal pre-existence of Jesus is simply incompatible with the reality of his human nature. This is not argued, but repeatedly asserted: "We can have the humanity without the pre-existence and we can have the pre-existence without the humanity. There is absolutely no way of having both."[1] I remarked in a previous lecture that Dr Gregor Smith dismissed with one sweeping phrase the whole tradition of natural theology; now we have Dr Knox dismissing with equal sublimity the whole of the classical Christology from Athanasius and Cyril (and many of their opponents) to Augustine and Aquinas and beyond. If (we may ask) the pre-existence of Jesus and his humanity are *a priori* incompatible, what on earth were the Christological controversies about? The great thinkers of the Christian Church may

[1] op. cit., p. 106.

have had their limitations, but they can hardly have been as incurably boneheaded as Dr Knox suggests. However, like other reductionists, Knox wishes to retain the traditional formulas, while giving them a meaning that Chalcedon would certainly have repudiated: "When we join the congregation in confessing the pre-existence, we are asserting, as we are bound by our own existence as Christians to do, that God, the Father Almighty, Maker of the heavens and the earth, was back of, present in, and acting through the whole event of which the human life of Jesus was the centre. We are saying that *God* was in Christ – not in the resurrection only, but in the whole of the human career from conception through death."[1] (An English reader has to remind himself here that in American English "through" means "up to and including", not as in British English "up to and beyond".) Surprisingly Knox denies that his position is adoptionist; the reason is apparently that for him the purpose of Christology is not in any case to make sense of the life of Jesus as it is recorded in the Gospels; it is to make sense of the experience of the primitive Church. What it does, and what the Church has done from the start, is to weave a pattern of myth around the figure of the earthly Jesus in order to provide a conceptual scheme for the Church's own experience. In spite of the way in which Knox speaks of the Church as having, in a somewhat "Pickwickian" sense, a "memory" of Jesus, it seems clear that for him

[1] ibid., p. 107.

the Gospels do not constitute in any sense a record of the witness of those who saw the deeds and heard the words of Jesus; what they are really *about* is not Jesus of Nazareth but the consciousness of primitive Christians. As far as Jesus himself is concerned, it is axiomatic that if he is fully human he cannot be, in anything other than a symbolic or pictorial sense, divine. Thus Knox tells us that to speak of God the Word as being made flesh in Christ "is by no means the same thing as identifying Jesus of Nazareth with this pre-existing, and always existing, hypostasis. Just as the reality of God is not exhausted in the Logos, yet is fully present in it, so the reality of the Logos was fully present in the Event of which the human life of Jesus was the centre and therefore pre-eminently in that human life itself, but without being simply identical with Jesus."[1] He says categorically that "it is impossible to conceive that God could become a man".[2]

It is perfectly clear that Dr Knox believes himself to be interpreting the classical Christian doctrine of the Incarnation and not to be putting something else in its place; it is equally clear to me that he is doing nothing of the sort. That this is so appears from the fact that, if he is right, it would have been idolatrous for the Apostles during the earthly life of Jesus to have given Jesus the worship which we now give him. Knox, by his own avowal, is not happy to say that the Word was incarnate in Jesus, but rather that "the Incarnation

[1] ibid., pp. 109f.   [2] ibid., p. 111.

took place in Jesus-in-the-midst-of-his-own – in other words, in the nascent Church".[1] This is not a matter of theological technicalities and hair-splitting; it strikes at the root of Christian discipleship, the giving to a man who was crucified in Palestine the unconditional allegiance which God alone can rightly receive. The assertions which Christians make at their baptism are no longer assertions about Jesus; "Jesus" becomes simply the model for the correlation and systematisation of the experience of the Christian Church, parallel to the way in which the concepts of atomic physics provide a model for the correlation and systematisation of certain physical phenomena. It is, I think, significant and disquieting that Dr Knox and those who think with him find it more congenial to talk about the "Christ-Event" than about the Person Christ; for how does one give personal allegiance to an *event*? An Englishman might have a genuine (though, it is to be hoped, a conditional and finite) devotion to Lord Nelson, but hardly to the Battle of Trafalgar. Plainly, Knox is striving to avoid entangling Christian belief with metaphysical concepts and systems; but, like so many of those who attempt this task, he uncritically accepts the assumptions of one particular contemporary metaphysical doctrine, in this case the doctrine that experience is the object and not just the medium of knowledge. (To preserve the Christian faith from contamination by metaphysics you need a metaphysician, not a non-metaphysician or an anti-

[1] ibid., p. 112.

metaphysician!) In asserting, as he does, without argument that the true humanity of Christ excludes his preexistence, Knox, as we have seen, brushes aside as unworthy of attention the whole tradition of Christological thought. It is significant, and a matter for gratitude, that while mythologising belief about Christ, Knox sees no need to mythologise belief about God; indeed, it is precisely because he understands "God" in the traditional metaphysical sense that he denies Jesus' metaphysical pre-existence. More thorough-going revisionists, such as van Buren, find no difficulty in saying (of course in a mythological sense) that Christ is God, because for them Christ and God are equally mythological. Dr Knox, however, appears to be running with the mythological Christological hare and following with the metaphysical theistic hounds. He is quite certainly doing his best to retain the traditional Christian attitude to Jesus. He even, stretching his own principles to the limit, can go as far as to speak of Jesus as divine, but only in the sense that his divinity is "a transformed, a redeemed and redemptive, humanity"[1]; but, while conceding the term "divinity" to Jesus, he noticeably avoids the term "deity". He explicitly asserts that what matters is not who Christ *was* but what was *happening* in him, and that nothing more can be required of a Christology than that it takes adequate account of the experience of the Church. I can only comment that a Christology which limits itself to taking adequate ac-

[1] ibid., p. 113.

count of the experience of the Church will be found in the end not to have taken adequate account of that experience. It is paradoxical that Knox, with his extreme emphasis upon the experience of the Church, finds himself unable to accept the Church's own account of the ground of that experience; this does, I think, suggest that the metaphysical, epistemological and methodological tools with which he has equipped himself are not really adequate for his task.

In discussing elsewhere Dr Knox's earlier book *The Church and the Reality of Christ* I characterised his position as one which reduced all theology to ecclesiastical psychology;[1] this seems to me to be equally true of the later work which I have just been discussing. To repeat what I then said:

> The attractiveness of Knox's position, as of other "reductionist" versions of Christianity, lies in its alleged immunity to the depredations of New-Testament scholars upon the factuality of the events described in the Gospels. I am not convinced that this is an immunity that Christianity either ought or needs to claim, and I would add that it is only a highly selective attitude to New-Testament scholars that produces the impression of depredation at all.[2]

One of the most helpful Christological discussions that

[1] E. L. Mascall, *The Secularisation of Christianity*, p. 256.
[2] ibid., p. 266.

has appeared in recent years is contained in Dr John Hick's essay "Christology at the Cross Roads" in the symposium *Prospect for Theology* which was published in 1966 as a *Festschrift* for Dr H. H. Farmer. Hick begins by pointing out that "the most disturbing theological problem that Christianity is likely to have to face corporately during the next hundred years or so . . . arises from the communicational unification of the world and the consequent emergence of a common human history. This", he continues, "has brought Christianity face to face with other world religions. . . . In this new situation the old issue of the uniqueness of the Christian revelation, and of the nature of the Christian claim over against other religions, has become urgent and may become obsessive." This problem of the uniqueness of Christianity Hick sees as intimately related to the problem of the uniqueness of Christ; he asserts that "it is on this most central and crucial issue that Christology stands today at the cross roads".[1] He remarks that the first and classic occurrence of debate about the precise nature of Christ's uniqueness was in the fourth century in the Arian controversy. "In modern times", he adds, "the issue has generally been defined as the question whether Christ's uniqueness was a uniqueness of kind or of degree; and it is the apparently growing tendency towards what I shall call a Degree or Neo-Arian Christology that I want to discuss . . . by referring to three of its recent representatives."[2]

[1]op. cit., p. 139.   [2]ibid., p. 140.

The three representatives whom he chooses are
Norman Pittenger, Nels Ferré and the late D. M.
Baillie. I cannot here discuss Hick's arguments in detail
and I shall simply list the three objections (very
weighty objections, in my opinion) which he brings
against any degree-Christology. First, he points out the
difficulty which such a Christology has in asserting or
defending the uniqueness of Christ; this is, of course, the
weakness which, earlier in this lecture, I saw in the
evolutionary Christology of Bethune-Baker. Secondly,
he sees a great deal in the New Testament which is
difficult to reconcile with a degree-Christology; John
Knox would, of course, agree, though he would not see
this as a weakness. Thirdly, Hick adduces the Athana-
sian argument that "no creature, however exalted,
could deputise for God in the salvation of mankind".[1]
In this connection he mentions D. M. Baillie's view of
the Incarnation as the supreme manifestation of the
grace of God. "This suggestion", he writes, "places incarnation at the top of a continuous scale which descends through saintliness to the ordinary levels of
human life. . . . Thus incarnation is a general feature of
human life, manifest in many different degrees and in a
vast range of concrete forms, among which the life of
Jesus is pre-eminent in the completeness with which the
human was freely interpenetrated by the divine."[2]
Hick is rather more sympathetic to Baillie's view than I
should be, mainly because he sees salvation primarily in

[1] ibid., p. 147.   [2] ibid., p. 148.

terms of obedience than of transformation; in a fuller discussion I should want to take issue with him on the notion of "deification", and this would lead into a major investigation of the doctrine of grace as it is variously understood in the Catholic, Orthodox and Protestant Churches. Nevertheless he comes down clearly against degree-Christologies. Whether or not it can be proved from the New Testament that Jesus claimed to be the eternal Son or Logos made flesh, this, he tells us, is

a claim that the Church has made for him, impelled by the inner logic of the worship that he has evoked by his redeeming influence upon human life. The Nicene-Chalcedonian definition of Christ as God incarnate springs from the same fundamental religious motive as the Anselmic definition of God as that than which no more perfect can be conceived. . . . The attitude of worship demands the absoluteness of its object; and the test of this absoluteness is whether the object really (i.e. legitimately) demands our worship. To confirm or disconfirm the Chalcedonian Christology we therefore have to return to the person of Jesus, as he meets us in the New Testament and in a faith evoked by the New Testament, to ask whether what he does for us and to us is such that we must respond, with doubting Thomas, "My Lord – and my God."[1]

[1] ibid., p. 149.

Having disposed, sympathetically but firmly, of the degree- or Neo-Arian Christology, Hick turns to the task of restating the Chalcedonian position in a way that can be intelligible today. "The main feature of the Nicene and Chalcedonian formularies that renders them unacceptable today is their central reliance on the category of substance. They assert that Jesus Christ had [should he not rather have said "has"?] two natures, being as human *homoousios* (of one substance) with mankind and as divine *homoousios* with the Godhead."[1] The chief objection to a substance-Christology in Hick's view is the static character of the notion of substance; he therefore tries to develop a more dynamic Christology in terms of the divine love or *Agapé*. "We may emphasise what the Chalcedonian formula was concerned to emphasise in its *homoousios* by saying that Jesus' *agapé* towards the men and women whom he met in Palestine was not *like* God's *Agapé* towards them (this would correspond to the Arian *homoiousios*), nor was it a reflection or imitation of the divine *Agapé*, but it actually and literally *was* God's *Agapé* acting towards them."[2]

Time will not permit me to describe in detail the way in which Hick attempts to construct an *Agapé*-Christology; it certainly does not enable him to avoid philosophical questions, and a large part of his exposition is devoted to investigating the difference between the qualitative and the numerical senses of identity. His conclusion is, in fact, very modest:

[1]ibid., p. 150.   [2]ibid., p. 155.

The assertion that Jesus' agapéing was continuous with the divine Agapéing is no more self-explanatory than the assertion that Christ was of one substance with the Father. Neither of these phrases, strictly speaking, explains anything. Each is concerned merely to point to a fact of faith; and each is concerned to point to the same fact of faith. But nevertheless I wish tentatively to suggest that the continuity-of-agapéing formulation may today be more intelligible than the oneness-of-substance formulation. Let us proclaim the *homoagapé* rather than the *homoousia*! For we know, at least ostensibly (and what better way could there be?), what we mean by *agapé*, but we do not know what we mean by substance – or at least, whatever meanings of "substance" we isolate we then have to disavow as failing to provide an interpretation of *homoousios* which would render that term acceptable, or even genuinely intelligible, to twentieth-century Christians – let alone twentieth-century non-Christians![1]

I find Dr Hick's essay extremely interesting and I only wish that I could discuss it at adequate length. Whether he is successful or not, his clear perception of the inadequacy of degree-Christology is both impressive and timely; so is his desire to restate the Chalcedonian Christology and not to substitute something else for it. I am not, however, convinced that he has succeeded. In

[1] ibid., pp. 165f.

spite of his determination, I am not sure that his *homo-agapé* preserves the deity of Jesus as does the *homoousios*, nor am I sure that it is really more intelligible to the twentieth-century Christian. If it is true, as I think it is, that, in the past, substance or *ousia* has been conceived in too static a manner, the remedy would seem to lie in conceiving it more dynamically rather than in abandoning it. We should, however, remember that power (*dynamis*) can be as inhuman as substance and indeed more so; while the famous definition of "person" as an individual substance of a rational nature shows that substance is not necessarily impersonal. If the objection is simply that to the ordinary non-expert man or woman substance will need a good deal of explaining, it might be replied that *agapé* will need even more. It was in any case a real advance when, round about the third century, the Church let the term *Logos* or "Word", as the name of the Second Person of the Trinity, fall into the background and brought into the limelight his personal name of "Son". However, if what we are seeking is a simple and untechnical way of stating the truth about the Incarnation, as distinct from theorising about it, I suggest that we could hardly do better than take two phrases from that somewhat neglected formulary the *Quicunque vult*, one of which consists in English entirely of monosyllables and the other almost entirely so. "Though he is God and man, he is not two but one Christ: one, not by Godhead being changed into flesh but by manhood being taken up into God." The implications of this are endless, but its statement could hardly be simpler.

If, now, we want to recover a more dynamic concept of the Incarnation we might well go back behind Chalcedon to Athanasius. The Chalcedonian formula gives a perfectly accurate statement of the *product* of the Incarnation: in the incarnate Lord there are two natures united in one person. In Athanasius, however, we have a much more explicit account of the *process*: in order to redeem man, the Son and Word of God, through whom the very universe had been made and by whom it is sustained, embraced human nature and became man. Gregory Dix once pointed out that for pre-Nicene theology in general the Incarnation was thought of not so much as due to the overshadowing of Mary by the Holy Spirit as to the assumption of human nature in her womb by the divine Logos himself; every pre-Nicene exegete interpreted the text of Luke i. 35 ("The Holy Ghost shall come upon thee . . .") as referring not to the Third Person of the Trinity but to the Second; this is true even of those to whom the distinction of the two Persons was most clear.[1] There is, of course, no essential contradiction between a process-Christology and a product-Christology; indeed each implies the other. So typical a "product-Christologist" as St Leo the Great finds it necessary to emphasise the process: "Lowliness was assumed by majesty, weakness by power, mortality by eternity."[2] And it is in terms of the

[1] G. Dix, *The Shape of the Liturgy*, p. 276.
[2] *Letter to Flavian* (the "Tome of Leo"), iii.

process that the nature of the Incarnation as *Heils-geschichte*, "salvation-history", is most evident; as I stressed in the last lecture, the taking of human nature by God the Son initiates the renewal of humanity itself, it brings about a real change in the human race. "When thou tookest upon thyself man to deliver him, thou didst not disdain a Virgin's womb." There has been in modern Christological writing a persistent tendency to insist in the most literal way on the humanity of Jesus and then to let the divinity take care of itself, so that the divinity is either explicitly denied or reinterpreted as perfect humanity or else given some other reduced meaning. Furthermore humanity tends to be seen as inherently subject to the same limitations and imperfections as those to which it is subject in any of us fallen men, and in consequence Jesus is alleged to have been not only ignorant, but positively mistaken and even sinful. Now it is, of course, important to affirm the concrete reality of the human nature of Jesus and there are certain limitations to which his human nature must be subject simply because it is finite and created. It is, however, quite another thing to take fallen human nature as the norm and to reduce deity to its dimensions. This is precisely that changing of the Godhead into flesh – and into fallen flesh at that – against which the *Quicunque vult* warns us. If, on the other hand, manhood is taken up into God, we may expect it to manifest quite unpredictable and unexpected powers and properties. The assumption of human nature by God the Son is in any case a profound mystery; as St Thomas Aquinas says, "of all the works of God the mystery of the Incarnation most greatly surpasses our reason; for nothing more wonderful could be thought of that God could do than that very God, the Son of God, should become very man.[1]" That it is possible at all tells us a great deal about human nature itself. It lines us up, on one issue at least, with Luther against Calvin, namely that the finite – at least when it is the *human* finite – has a capacity for the infinite; though it would perhaps be more accurate to say neither *finitum capax infiniti* nor *finitum non capax infiniti*, but rather *infinitus capax finiti*, since it is the finite term – human nature – which is embraced and transformed by the infinite. And here we must recall a point made earlier in these lectures, that finite being is, by the very fact of its finitude and un-self-sufficiency, open towards the Creator on whom, for its very existence, it depends. And in manhood, which is not merely finite but is also personal, there will be unique possibilities in this openness to a Creator who is himself personal. One of such possibilities is the elevation of finite human beings into the life of God himself which is described as the action of grace; another – though we might never have dreamt of it ourselves – is the assumption of a human life by God himself in the Incarnation, and this is even more wonderful. In St Thomas's words, nothing more wonderful could be thought of that God could do. To quote the *Quicunque*

[1] *Summa contra Gentiles*, IV, xxvii.

vult again, "the right faith is that we believe and con-
fess that our Lord Jesus Christ, the Son of God, is God
and man: God of the substance of the Father, begotten
before the worlds, and man of the substance of his
mother, born in the world: perfect God and perfect
man". That is to say, he is not literally man but God
only in a reduced sense, as the kenoticists hold; nor is he
literally God but only apparently man, as the docetics
held. He is literally God and literally man. I have said
that the *possibility* of this tells us a great deal about what
human nature is; we can now add that the *actuality* of
this – the fact that it has, in fact, taken place – tells us a
great deal about what human beings can become. He
has become what we are in order that we should become what he is. An unforgettable collect prays that,
as he became partaker of our humanity, we may become partakers of his divinity. And all this is possible,
without our ceasing to be creatures, simply because to
be a creature is to be open to God, and to be a personal
creature is to be capable of a personal union with a
personal God.

There are, of course, a great many theological
problems arising out of the assumption of human nature
by God. In particular there are the problems of the
character and limitations of the human psyche of Jesus,
the problems which have almost completely dominated
the Christology of the last century. They do not seem
to me to be the really important problems, nor do I
think they are capable of solution in the terms in which

they are usually set. It is surely futile to ask what it feels like to be God incarnate. What we see when we look at the Gospels – and I must refer you to my book *The Secularisation of Christianity*[1] for a fuller discussion of this – is a picture of a completely unified life which is being lived on two levels at the same time. The argument is that "a narrative which, without any suggestion of incoherence, can be read as either an extremely earthy human story or as a highly theological document, and this without in any way losing its unity, derives this extraordinary character not from the fact that its author was a literary genius of the highest order but from the fact that it is recording the impact made upon his beholders by someone who, while he was a completely unified Person, was nevertheless, in the unity of his person, fully human and truly divine".[2] If we wish to probe into the character of the incarnate life of the divine Son we shall, I think, find Fr Karl Rahner's discussions as illuminating as any.[3] but I do not think this is the central issue of Christology. The central issue, as I see it, is concerned with what the assumption of human nature by God the Son at a moment of human history has done for mankind, and for the universe of which mankind is part; and, as we saw in the last lecture, it is here that Teilhard de Chardin, with all his weaknesses, has so much to teach us. And here I must

[1] op. cit., pp. 237ff.   [2] ibid., p. 244.
[3] K. Rahner, *Theological Investigations*, I, ch. v; IV, ch. iv; V, chs. viii, ix.

emphasise that, paradoxical as it may appear at first sight, it is only in the light of the orthodox Christology that we can make that positive and synthetic evaluation of the non-Christian religions which, as we saw earlier in this lecture, was discerned by Dr John Hick as constituting the most crucial and urgent task for Christian theology in the immediate future. For it is only if Christ is metaphysically, and not merely comparatively, unique, only if he is different in kind and not merely in degree from other great religious prophets and teachers, that we can significantly ask the question: What was Christ himself doing in those religions? Vatican II has given us a splendid lead here, both in the Constitution on the Church and in the Declaration on the Relationship of the Church to non-Christian Religions. "The Catholic Church", the latter document affirms, "rejects nothing which is true and holy in these religions. She looks with sincere respect upon those ways of conduct and of life, those rules and teachings, which, though differing in many particulars from what she holds and sets forth, nevertheless often reflect a ray of that Truth which enlightens all men."[1] Such a statement as this, however, only initiates the task, and it is precisely because it is pointing to a realm of theology that is still only in its beginnings that, compared with some of the other documents of the Council, this Declaration is both brief and sketchy. Among English-speaking scholars who have done valuable work in this

[1] op. cit., n. 2.

sphere I would mention specially Professor R. C. Zaehner of Oxford and Dr Geoffrey Parrinder of King's College, London, the former a Roman Catholic and the latter a Methodist, both of whom have attempted not merely to achieve an accurate and sympathetic understanding of the great world-religions but also to make a positive assessment of the place which they hold in relation to the redemption of mankind by Christ. So far as the great pre-Christian religions are concerned – Judaism, Hinduism, Buddhism, Zoroastrianism, Confucianism, Taoism – there is no special difficulty in seeing them all as, in their different ways, genuine, if partial and often distorted, revelations of God and preparations for the Gospel, though this still leaves for investigation the really vital problem of what God was actually doing in and through each of them, considered not just as a system of thought but as a concrete fact and process in the history of mankind. In the case of Islam – the one great world-religion which has arisen since the Incarnation – a special problem presents itself, as Professor Zaehner has pointed out:[1] how can there be a revelation, even a partial and distorted one, given through Mohammed if the full and final revelation had *already* been given in Jesus Christ? It is to problems such as these that the Christian student of comparative theology will need to give his attention and one cannot forecast what the answers will be. What is at least clear is that Christological thought in the future

[1] *The Catholic Church and World Religions*, ch. iii.

will have to take place in a much wider perspective than in the past, a perspective which is as wide as the human race and, indeed, as wide as the created universe. For we cannot even limit the redemptive work of Christ to this planet. There may be, for all we know, in some other part or parts of the universe than our own, rational corporeal beings other than man. If there are, they may or may not have sinned. If they have sinned, their redemption may or may not require that the Son of God should become incarnate in their nature as he has become incarnate in ours. God may or may not have some other way of restoring them to himself; he may perhaps have an even more wonderful way, of which we cannot form the remotest conception.[1] On matters such as these we can speculate, but can do little more. What we must never lose from sight is the fact that, from the moment of his taking flesh in the womb of Mary, God the Son has been the subject of a created human nature. "When thou tookest upon thyself man to deliver him, thou didst not disdain a Virgin's womb." We may recall the stirring words of the Constitution on the Divine Liturgy:

> Christ Jesus, the High Priest of the new and eternal Covenant, by taking human nature, introduced into this earthly exile that hymn which is sung throughout all ages in the halls of heaven. He joins the entire

[1] Cf. the discussion in my *Christian Theology and Natural Science*, pp. 36ff.

community of mankind to himself, and associates it with his own singing of this canticle of divine praise. For he continues his priestly work through the agency of his Church, which is ceaselessly engaged in praising the Lord and interceding for the salvation of the whole world.[1]

And, in the even more glorious words of the Epistle to the Colossians:

He is the image of the unseen God
and the first-born of all creation,
for in him were created
all things in heaven and on earth:
everything visible and everything invisible,
Thrones, Dominations, Sovereignties, Powers –
all things were created through him and for him.
Before anything was created, he existed,
and he holds all things in unity.
Now the Church is his body,
he is its head.

As he is the Beginning,
he was first to be born from the dead,
so that he should be first in every way;
because God wanted all perfection

[1]op. cit., n. 83.

to be found in him
and all things to be reconciled through him and for him,
everything in heaven and everything on earth,
when he made peace
by his death on the cross.[1]

[1] Col. i. 15–20 (Jerusalem Bible version).

CHAPTER FIVE

The Question of the Church

"FOR THE CATHOLIC CHRISTIAN '*Quid vobis videtur de Ecclesia, What think ye of the Church?*' is not merely as pertinent a question as '*Quid vobis videtur de Christo, What think ye of the Christ?*': it is but the same question differently formulated."[1] When these words were written in 1926 by the great Anglican Biblical scholar Sir Edwyn Hoskyns they came, I think, with a certain air of novelty if not of paradox even to the Catholic Christian who could hardly deny their truth when they were brought to his notice. Émile Mersch's magisterial work *Le Corps mystique du Christ* was not to appear until 1933, and the great movement of ecclesiological thought and writing which was to culminate in the Constitution *Lumen Gentium* of Vatican II had hardly come to birth. Except in those circles in which the Church was conceived as an entirely invisible entity, it was almost invariably thought of as an organisation, even if an organisation of a unique type and bearing a divine commission; and controversies about the Church were predominantly concerned with its structure, its governmental organs and their authority. Behind this there lay, of course, a long history stretching back to the time of the

[1] E. C. Hoskyns, "The Christ of the Synoptic Gospels", in E. G. Selwyn (ed.), *Essays Catholic and Critcal*, p. 153.
J

Reformation and, behind that, to the Middle Ages.
The struggles between Popes and Emperors and between Popes and Councils, the revolts of Wycliffe, Luther
and Calvin, the conflicts in England between Episcop-
alians, Presbyterians and Independents were all, so far
as their public form was concerned, the expression of
diverse beliefs about the way in which the Church was
meant to be organised and governed. Little attention, if
any, was given to the question of what the Church *is*.
The prorogation of Vatican I, immediately after its decree on the Papacy, only hardened this impression, and
even in the nineteen-fifties it was possible for Mgr (now
Cardinal) Journet to take in hand an exhaustive treatise
on the Church which opened with a systematic and detailed exposition of the hierarchy as constituting the
efficient cause of the Church. Nevertheless, the conviction was steadily growing that, important as the
organisational and governmental aspect of the Church
might be, it was an expression and manifestation of the
Church's life and being, and not that life and being itself. The movement which Mersch and those who
thought with him had initiated grew steadily, in spite of
occasional aberrations of an almost gnostic or pantheis-
tic type. It received authoritative, if to some extent ad-
monitory, endorsement in 1943, in Pope Pius XII's
encyclical *Mystici Corporis Christi*. In its more recent
phases this "body-of-Christ" ecclesiology has had to
compete with a rival ecclesiology for which the de-
fining mark of the Church is its character as the People

of God. The two ecclesiologies are, however, complementary rather than antagonistic, and both are in marked contrast with the quasi-military notion of the Church which was characteristic of the Counter-Reformation. It must be stressed that the notion of the People of God, while it gives clear expression to the fact that the Church is a society of human beings, is not a merely social concept. It has behind it all the Old-Testament teaching that the people Israel is the bride of the Lord Jehovah, with whom he has made a covenant and to whom he has given a law by which to live, and it sees this doctrine, which is unfulfilled in the Old Testament itself, as fulfilled and transformed in the New Covenant, sealed in the blood of Christ the world's Redeemer, through which Israel, the People of God, is thrown open to the entire human race. To avoid any crude quasi-political doctrine of the Church, Vatican II, in the Constitution on the Church *Lumen Gentium*, opened its exposition with a chapter on the Church as a divine mystery and only after this proceeded to develop the notion of the Church as the People of God. In following this course the Council was acting in accordance with its twin principles of speaking to the world in language that the world would be able to understand and of giving its teaching the widest possible foundation in Scripture. It must, however, be noticed that, within this global notion of the people of God, the fact that the Church is Christ's body was given clear expression; this is, if anything, even more prominent in the theological paragraphs of the Constitution on the Divine Liturgy.

In spite of this welcome recasting and development it can hardly be denied that this renewed emphasis upon the specifically *religious* character of the Church has often had an unpleasantly negative and exclusive tone. An Anglican participant in a great ecumenical gathering in the inter-war period remarked that serious obstacles arose from the fact that, while the Eastern Orthodox present would hear nothing bad about the Church, the Lutherans would hear nothing good about the world. And it must be admitted that, in other religious confessions than these two, the Church has often been exalted at the expense of mankind as a whole. The Church is indeed open to the whole of mankind, but what about that part of mankind – the major part in fact – which, whether culpably or inculpably, has not come in? Are they simply in outer darkness, whether or not they are gnashing their teeth? Is there not an accepted theological principle *Extra ecclesiam nulla salus,* "There is no salvation outside the Church"? If the Church is the People of God and the Body of Christ, whose people and whose body are those who are outside? Can we, in fact, extol the Church without despising the world? These are genuinely serious questions for Christians in these days when improved communications have brought men of all faiths and cultures into ever-increasing proximity and when the researches of scholars have made it more and more difficult for us to dismiss the non-Christian religions as merely conglomerations of confusion and falsehood.

We are, I would suggest, in danger of an error to which Christians have only too often been prone, the error of supposing that we can extol the greater only by deprecating the lesser. A notable example of this is the fear felt by many that if we give to Mary and the saints the honour that is due to them we shall be exalting them above the level of honour which belongs to God alone. Now it may, of course, be the case that if we give to Mary and the saints the honour that is due to them we shall be exalting them above God *as we conceive him*, but this can only be because we have a pitifully low concept of God himself. It is surely more fruitful to give them the honour which is their due and then to say, in the words of Faber's hymn:

> If Mary is so beautiful,
> What must her Maker be?

So then, instead of starting from the Church and then concluding that the rest of mankind is a sheer mass of perdition, we shall do better first to think of the relation of God and Christ to mankind as a whole and then to see what is to be said about their special relation to the Church. It is this principle of *Quo majus*, of "How much more", that I propose to follow.

What then, from the Christian point of view, is the basic fact about the human race? It is that it is created

and preserved and illuminated by the eternal Son and
Word of God, the Second Person of the Holy Trinity.
"All things were made by him," the prologue of St
John's Gospel declares, "and without him nothing was
made. What was made was life in him, and the life was
the light of men."[1] This is itself a tremendous and in-
spiring truth about the whole of mankind, which should
lead us to approach the religions of the world with respect and sympathy, and indeed with humility. There is,
however, more to come. "To as many as received him he
gave power to become children of God, those who believe in his name. . . . And the Word became flesh and
dwelt among us (and we beheld his glory, glory as of the
Father's only-begotten), full of grace and truth."[2] I
shall not try to settle here the disputed question whether
the Evangelist is saying here that those who received the
Word outside the Judaeo-Christian revelation were
potentially sons of God or whether he is speaking of the
actual sonship of those who know and accept him explicitly. What I wish to emphasise is, first, that all mankind is illuminated by the light of the eternal Word,
who has made it and sustains it in his own image,
whether it opens itself to that light or not; and, secondly,
that the taking of human nature by the Word has made
a real and irreversible difference to the whole human

[1] John i. 3, 4. The alternative punctuation, giving the reading
". . . nothing was made that was made. In him was life . . .", does
not materially alter the meaning.
[2] John i. 12, 14.

race and, beyond that, to the whole material universe of which man is part. Human existence and human history can never be the same again since the moment when God the Son united human nature to himself in a union which will never be dissolved. It will be one of the tasks of the theology of the future to work out the implications of this amazing truth, for, apart from occasional adumbrations in such fathers as St Irenaeus, the theology of the past, especially in the West, has paid little attention to it. Furthermore, as several theologians have remarked recently, more attention needs to be given to the fact that it is not just any one of the three divine Persons that has become incarnate, but the Second Person, the Son. It is not simply that *God* has become man in order to make us partakers of his *Godhead*, but that *the Son* has become man in order that we might be partakers of his *sonship;* that we should have power to become the *children* of God.[1] Thus a real, even if an inchoate and diffused, transformation of the material realm, and in particular of the human race, was inaugurated by the incarnation of the eternal Son of God in human flesh and blood. Man, by the very fact of his creation in the image of God, has the potentiality of sharing in the sonship of him who is inherently and by right both the eternal Son and the perfect image of the Father; when the Son embraced human nature in the womb of Mary and himself became man, that potentiality began to be actualised. Our human condition can

[1] Cf. K. Rahner, *Theological Investigations*, IV, ch. iv.

never be the same again, either in this world or beyond the grave. In the thrilling words of St Thomas Aquinas, "It is no longer incredible that a creature's intellect should be capable of union with God by beholding the divine essence, since the time when God became united to man by taking a human nature to himself."[1] We may indeed speculate that, if mankind had not previously fallen away from God by sin, the assumption of human nature by the eternal Son might have been the simultaneous assumption of the whole human race into him, its incorporation into his sonship and into his vision of the Father. However that may be, the hard fact is that man has fallen away from God and that his restoration to true sonship requires not only the assumption of human nature by the eternal Son but also the living out by the Son in that human nature of a perfect human life. This is not the place for a discussion of the manner and operation of Christ's work of redemption, of the necessity that he should die and rise again from death before the full efficacy of his incarnation could be released. This necessity should not lead us to ignore the fact that the renewal and regeneration of the human race began when the Word became flesh and dwelt among us. In the words of the Ambrosian hymn:

> *Aequalis aeterno Patri,*
> *carnis tropaeo accingere,*
> *infirma nostri corporis*
> *virtute firmans perpeti.*
> [1]*Comp. Theol.*, 201.

Eternal as the Father thou,
Gird on our flesh for victory now;
The weakness of our mortal state
With deathless might invigorate.

But now, having insisted on the fact that in the Incarnation of the eternal Son something of tremendous import happened not merely *for* but *to* the human race, we must now turn to the fact that, when in his Ascension the incarnate Son had withdrawn his personal visibility from us, he created and commissioned a new visible manifestation of his presence in the sacramental body, the one, holy, catholic and apostolic Church. If we are asked why this was needed and why the regeneration of the human race might not have been brought to completion by the gradual expansion and burgeoning of the change which had been made in mankind at its root by the simple fact of the assumption of human nature by the Son, we must, I think, reply that, in so far as we are able to pry into the counsels of the Almighty, it was, if not absolutely necessary, at least fitting and desirable that the re-created human race should be seen to be a *people*, a renewed and redeemed society, at the same time a pledge and an anticipation of the total renewal and redemption of the human race. And this means that the Church is not simply a community of those who have been snatched out of a sinful world and are now safely incapsulated in an impermeable membrane, so that they can neither affect nor be affected by anything that is going on outside. They are to be the medium from which the renewing and redemptive power of Christ is to be communicated to the world, and there is thus a constant osmosis in both directions between the Church and the world. Thus it is that, in spite of their theoretical distinctness, there is a fundamental inter-permeation of the Church and the world; not only is the redemptive power passing from the Church to the world and transforming the world into the Church, but also the egotism and voracity of a fallen world is passing into the Church and distorting its true nature. This is the glory and the shame of the Church. The wheat and the tares must grow together until the harvest, however certain it may be that the tares will not stifle and destroy the wheat. We might well remind ourselves of these words of St. Augustine:

> If you belong to Christ's members, come inside, keep close to the Head. Put up with the tares if you are wheat. Put up with the chaff if you are grain. Put up with the bad fish if you are a good fish. Why do you fly away before the winnowing? Why do you root up the grain with yourself before the harvest? Why do you rend the nets before you have come to the shore?[1]

The fundamental relation of the Church to the world is splendidly expressed in these words of Bishop Christopher Butler:

[1] *In Psal. xl.*

Not only do we believe that the God of our salvation is the creator of the world and of every man. We believe that the redemption wrought in Christ is of universal significance; that it has changed the basic relation of man, as man, with God. We can suppose, with K. Rahner,[1] that the "possibility" of the actual creation as we know it depends on the "possibility" of the incarnation, and that the Word made flesh is the ultimate source, as it were the transcendent dimension, of man's very existence as man. The Church, in fact, exists to bring a message and means of redemption to a redeemed world; just as we have been taught by St Paul that she exists, in her members, in virtue of a lifelong "mortification" of that "old man" which has already been "put to death" in them through baptism.[2]

Thus the Church of Christ is not only the redeemed but also the redemptive community, the presence of Christ in the world. We might express this by saying that the world is to become formally the Church, while the Church is to become materially the world; that is to say, that it is the function of the Church, or perhaps we should say it is the purpose of Christ through his body the Church, to bring the whole world, healed, purged and reorientated, within that perfect human offering of manhood to the Father which Christ made once and

[1] *Nature and Grace*, p. 23.
[2] *The Theology of Vatican II*, p. 187.

for all on Calvary and which he perpetuates in heaven. Thus the sacraments, and indeed the whole life of the Church in liturgy, prayer and service, have a two-fold function: both to preserve and amplify the Church as the redeemed people of God and also to be the redeeming instrument of Christ through which the world may be brought to God. Even those aspects of the Church's life which are materially most remote from the world's affairs must, if they are to be fruitful and not to go sour on themselves, be consciously related to the world as a whole. The prayer of the enclosed religious, the pain of a bed-ridden sufferer, the liturgical worship of the Christian congregation, the performance by Christian men and women of their daily duties patiently and conscientiously, all such activities of the Body of Christ and of its members will be fruitful for the sanctification of the individual Christians concerned in them if they are pursued not simply for the sanctification of the individual, nor even for the Church itself considered as a closed and compact organisation, but for the emancipation and transfiguration of the world. From the standpoint of canon law the Church may be *societas perfecta*, a tidily ordered and self-sufficient society, but from the standpoint of theology she can never be that while one single human being remains outside. The concern of the sacramental life of the Church with the transformation of man as such and of the universe of which he is part has rarely been to the forefront in Western theology, whether Catholic or Protestant, though it has, of course, achieved tumultuous expression in the writings of Pierre Teilhard de Chardin. It has been much more common in Eastern Orthodoxy; the following sentence of Paul Evdokimov is typical:

> The formation of Christ in man, his "Christification", is neither the impossible imitation nor the application to man of the merits of the Incarnation, but the projection into man of the Incarnation itself, operated and perpetuated by the Eucharistic mystery.[1]

Here, then, there are two great themes for investigation and elaboration by the theology of the future: first, the change brought about in human nature, and in the human situation as a whole, by the fact of the Incarnation of the Son of God; secondly, the relation of the sacramental life of the Church as the redeemed and redemptive Body of Christ to the world outside the Church's visible boundaries.

Limits of space and time will allow only brief mention of the vast range of new problems for the theology of the Church which have been made acute by the birth and growth of the Ecumenical Movement. Ten years ago it would have appeared obvious to most people that the Roman Church was most unlikely to enter actively into the Movement and that if it did the effects on the movement could only be that of a gigantic and catastrophic take-over bid. (It may be noted in

[1] *L'Orthodoxie*, p. 113.

passing that one distinguished Protestant professor has seen the participation of Anglicanism in the Movement as a similar take-over bid by Anglicanism for Protestantism.) It is therefore gratifying to observe that both these forecasts have been falsified in the most remarkable and welcome way. Not only has the Roman Church since Vatican II committed itself to ecumenism on the widest possible scale but it has shown a great readiness to reopen theological issues positively and constructively.

In the past an Anglican had usually looked to Eastern Orthodoxy for an ecclesiological outlook that was unaffected by both the juridicism of the Middle Ages and the individualism of the sixteenth century. I can record with gratitude that it was my introduction to the thought and worship of Orthodoxy as a young student in 1927 that showed me something wider than the rather provincial and antiquarian high-church Anglicanism which had itself come as a liberation from an intense but even narrower low-church variety. A closer acquaintance with Orthodoxy showed that some of the features of it which were most immediately attractive were themselves accretions of bygone ages, while it was nevertheless clear that something very authentic lay in the depths. As for Roman Catholicism, that, of course, was fettered forever to Trent and the Counter-Reformation. Recent developments have given the lie to any such judgment, and the common assumption that "Rome will never change" has given place to a sometimes more disturbing feeling that "You never know what Rome will do next". It would be unbecoming of me to express an opinion here about some of the more spectacular expressions of post-conciliar Roman Catholic thought and action. I may, however, offer a few comments on some of the central ecclesiological issues which have come to the forefront.

First one must place the recognition of the supreme ecclesiological significance of baptism. At the Congress on the Renewal of the Church, at Toronto in August 1967, Cardinal Suenens impressed on his audience the fact that the greatest day in the life of the Pope was neither the day of his election to the Papacy nor that of his coronation, but that of his baptism, when something happened to him which has happened to every other member of the Church. The readiness to give practical expression to this recognition is made clear in the provisions of the recent regulations prohibiting indiscriminate conditional rebaptism of Christians joining the Roman Communion from other churches. Together with this goes the recognition that a genuine, if not easily definable, ecclesial character attaches to all recognisably Christian communions. Special problems are raised by those communions in which baptism is either non-existent or optional, and quite different ones by a communion such as the Anglican, which claims to have a valid episcopate and presbyterate which Rome officially denies. Most significant is the attitude taken up by the Decrees of Vatican II on Ecumenism and the

Catholic Eastern Churches, from which it seems to be clear that the Eastern Churches separated from Rome, the validity of whose ordinations Rome has never questioned, are accepted as having fully ecclesial reality and authority. It is noteworthy that Rome is more ready than they are for occasional acts of eucharistic intercommunion, since to most Orthodox intercommunion presupposes a complete unity of faith which they see to be lacking in view of the Roman doctrines of the *filioque* and the Papal supremacy. Certainly the attitude of Rome to the Eastern Churches, as expressed in the conciliar and post-conciliar documents, seems to carry two consequences: first, that, however true and important the common Roman teaching about the papal supremacy may be, its non-acceptance by a Christian communion does not in itself prevent that communion from being a fully operative part of the true Church; secondly, that there is no theological necessity for the papal primacy to have anything approximating to the detailed and authoritarian character in relation to every part of the Church and every one of the faithful, that it has acquired in the Roman communion since the breach with the East or even since the third century. And this may be of very considerable practical importance in the ecumenical field, and not least in relation to Anglicanism.

For Anglicans at least there is great significance, both theoretical and practical, in the teaching of Vatican II on episcopal collegiality. It is, of course, well known that to the more conservative fathers of the Council, the whole notion of collegiality was abhorrent and that to many it seemed clearly inconsistent with the doctrine of the Papacy promulgated at Vatican I. Chapter iii of the Constitution on the Church bears clear marks of this disagreement, with the continual insertion of reminders that the episcopal *collegium* functions "always with" and "never without" the successor of Peter. Much may depend ecumenically on the final resolution of this point. It certainly seems difficult to see much difference between the description of an acceptable papacy given by the Archbishop of Canterbury in his widely read book *The Gospel and the Catholic Church* and the interpretation of the doctrine of Vatican II on the papacy in Bishop Christopher Butler's recent book *The Theology of Vatican II*. But, in much the same way as that in which Dr Karl Barth, having discovered to his surprise that his own belief about Justification was identical with that of the Council of Trent as interpreted by Dr Hans Küng, expressed some anxiety as to the extent to which Roman Catholic theologians in general would accept Dr Küng's interpretation,[1] so in the case of the papal primacy an Anglican may need some assurance that Bishop Butler's interpretation will be, if not the only one, at least the dominant one in the Roman Catholic Church of the future. If this should come about, one very substantial barrier between Rome and Anglicanism will have been removed.

[1] H. Küng, *Justification*, p. xx (Letter from K. Barth).

K

The concept of collegiality was brought into prominence by Vatican II in order to balance and co-ordinate the papacy and the episcopate, but it would seem to admit of extension throughout the Church's structure if the radically organic nature of the People of God is to be given full expression in practice. There are indeed suggestions of this in the decrees of the Council on the Bishops, the Priests and the Laity. There would appear to be some kind of analogy between the relation of the Pope to the Bishops, the relation of the Bishop to his Presbyters, and the relation of the Pastor to his Layfolk, though the differences between these must be at least as marked as their similarity.[1] Furthermore, for the healthy life of the body there would seem to be needed a widespread embodiment of the principle of subsidiarity, according to which nothing should be done at the higher level of a human society that can be done equally well at a lower one, for in this way there will be maximum room for the free expression of individual maturity and responsibility. Although there appears to be no explicit appeal to the principle of subsidiarity, it is clearly implied by the Council's call for a large measure of decentralisation, which has now begun to come into effect.

Again, the concept of the Church as the Body of Christ may go far towards removing the deadlock between Catholicism and Protestantism on the subject of

[1] Cf. E. L. Mascall, "Collegiality, Reunion and Reform", *Theology*, LXIX (1966), pp. 201ff, 255ff.

priesthood. Ever since the Reformation the Catholic insistence on the priestly character of the ordained presbyter has been met from the Protestant side either by an uncompromising denial that there is any priest except Christ or by an equally emphatic assertion of the priesthood of all believers. Vatican II has drawn together the elements of truth in all three positions by making it plain that, in the Christian dispensation, the only efficacious and underivative priesthood is that of Christ and that all other priesthood is simply a participation in his. It does, admittedly, affirm that the priesthood of the whole Church and the priesthood of the ordained presbyter differ in essence and not only in degree, but it explicitly states that this difference arises from different modes of participation in the one priesthood of Christ.[1] Both the priesthood of the Church and the sacrifice of the Eucharist are seen as derivative from the priesthood and the sacrifice of Christ, and this should allay the misgivings of any Protestants except those who maintain that both the priesthood and the sacrifice of Christ are things of the past which came to an end on Calvary.

At this point in the argument a shift of perspective is essential. From all that has been said hitherto it might appear that the Church, for all its dependence upon the ascended Christ, was simply a society on earth with a constantly changing composition, as new members entered it by baptism and old ones left it by death. This

[1] *Const. de Ecclesia*, n. 10.

would mean that the Church which is Christ's body and the Church militant on earth were not only essentially, but also numerically, identical. Even those who would formally repudiate this identification can only too easily slip into it in practice, and even in such an august and systematic document as the encyclical *Mystici Corporis* the assumption is silently made. Vatican II skilfully restores the balance in the chapter headed "The Pilgrim Church's Eschatological Character and her Union with the Church in Heaven".[1]

> Until the Lord comes in his glory and all the angels with him, and death is destroyed and all things have been put in subjection under him, some of his disciples are pilgrims on earth, some, their life now over, are undergoing purification, others are in their glory gazing "clearsighted on God himself, three in one, as he is". Despite the difference of our degree and mode, all of us are in communion with the same love of God and of our neighbour; we all sing the same hymn to the glory of our God. All who belong to Christ and are in possession of his Spirit, combine to make one church with a cohesion that depends on him.[2]

In order to show how, as I see the matter, this shift of perspective bears upon both our understanding of the Church and of its ministry, I will venture to quote a fairly extensive passage from my book *Corpus Christi*;

[1] *Const. de Ecclesia*, cap. vii.   [2] ibid., n. 49.

the passage in question is in an essay entitled "The One Church".

The part of the Church which is militant here on earth is only the fringe or the outpost of the whole Catholic Church of Christ. . . . Only too often the Church has been thought of as a purely earthly society, which we enter by baptism and leave by death, a continuing terrestrial organism with a constantly changing membership, comparable in this respect to the Royal College of Surgeons, or the Worshipful Company of Fishmongers. On such a view the Episcopate also is a group with a constantly changing membership, like the governing bodies of the two societies just mentioned, and if the bishops are conceived as having any relation to the apostles at all, it is merely the relation of being the apostles' successors. Now I do not deny that the phrase "apostolic succession" can be given a legitimate meaning; one bishop succeeds another bishop in his see, and each bishop is consecrated at the hands of other bishops. But the natural suggestions of the phrase seem to me to be highly misleading; it suggests that the episcopal office is like a relay-race in which each runner drops out when he has handed on his baton, and it gives some colour to the Protestant accusation that the Catholic view of the ministry is magical and materialistic. The truth, however, is that, although the Church has an earthly part which we call the Church militant, it is not just an earthly reality, and the Church militant at any particular epoch is only a minute fraction of the Church catholic. The Church's membership does indeed change as time goes on, but it changes simply by increasing. Men enter the Church by baptism; they do not leave it by death. And what is true of the Church is true of the apostolic Episcopate; a man enters the Episcopate by consecration, but he does not leave it by death. The Church grows with the passage of time, and the Episcopate grows within it. Thus a newly consecrated bishop is not in the strict sense a *successor* of the apostles; he is simply a new apostle. The church militant is, of course, the only part of the Church through which a man can enter into either the Church itself or its Apostolate; there are not, I imagine, baptisms or ordinations in either purgatory or heaven. This does not, however, affect the fact that the Church into which a man is baptised is not the Church militant but the whole Church of God, and that the ministry into which a man is ordained is not just the ministry of the Church militant, but the universal Apostolate.[1]

To adopt this supra-terrestrial view of the Church does not enable us to solve in one sweep all the problems of ecclesiology, but it does enable us to see them in a new light and in different proportions from those in which they commonly appear. It gives a more realistic under-

[1] *Corpus Christi*, 2nd ed., pp. 21f.

standing of the Communion of Saints; the saints are seen to be not our predecessors but our contemporaries. It makes it easier for us to see that the Church's ministry is *within* the Church and not just *over* it, and that the ministry is related to the Church in a way comparable to that in which the organs of a growing body are related to the body as a whole. It enables us to understand the Church's history not as a succession of episodes played out in an odd, and often very perverse, organisation, but as the growth of a supra-terrestrial organism of which the earthly Church is simply the lowest and most recently acquired fringe. We have, in fact, the picture of the Church as a living pyramid, whose apex is Christ, whose levels are composed of the successive generations which were once on earth and are now beyond the grave and whose base at any moment consists of the present generation of the earthly Church, which will pass in due course beyond the grave itself as the new base comes into being beneath it. All images and illustrations have, of course, their limitations and must be used with circumspection and restraint, but this one has, I think, special advantages. It keeps the Church triumphant and expectant constantly in view and stresses its living union with the Church on earth. It provides for the fundamentally *pilgrim* character of the earthly Church and, in line with the chapter of *De Ecclesia* from which I quoted earlier in this lecture, it includes a coherent eschatology which is both realised and futurist. And, because it sees the element of *suc-*

cession in the earthly Church as subsumed within a deeper and more embracing character of *incorporation* into the Church as a totality, it frees the doctrine of the sacraments and of the ministry from the suspicion of magic and of tyranny which it has often understandably carried with it. It enables us to avoid a crude and quasi-political triumphalism and at the same time to extol the Bride of the Lamb, the new and heavenly Jerusalem, who descends to earth from heaven in as much as earth itself is taken up into heaven in her. It does not seal off the Church in this world from the world in which it is situated; quite the opposite. But it sees the earthly Church, *sponsa Christi quae orbem militat ecclesia*, against the background of the Church triumphant and expectant; and it sees the warfare in which it is engaged not as a war *against* the world which God has created and for which his Son died, but as a war *for* the world against all the forces that alienate it from God and divide it within itself. I hope I shall not be accused of either utopianism or triumphialism if I recall in this context a stanza from a poem in which that eccentric and tragic, but marvellously perceptive, Christian Francis Thompson addressed the Church under the figure of the Lily of the King:

> O Lily of the King! I shall not see, that sing,
>   I shall not see the hour of thy queening!
> But my song shall see, and wake like a flower that
>   dawn winds shake,

And sigh with joy the odours of its meaning.
O Lily of the King, remember then the thing
    That this dead mouth sang; and thy daughters
As they dance before His way, sing there on the Day
What I sang when the Night was on the waters![1]

And now, having come to the end of this course of
lectures, I must try to indicate briefly the attitude in
which, as a Christian theologian in this year of grace
1968, I find myself facing the future. The present time
is, for theology as for the life of the Church and of the
world in general, a time of change, questioning and un-
certainty. This is in itself no valid ground for dismay. If
theologians are in any degree in touch with the world in
which they theologise, it is only to be expected that,
when the world is in a state of more than usual fluidity
and instability, theologians will find themselves faced
with novel and intricate questions. And, theologians
themselves being only finite beings, whose intelligence
is limited and whose judgment is often biased, it is not
surprising if in their weaker moments they find themselves hankering after the fleshpots of an imagined more
stable and peaceful theological past. Whether they
would, in fact, have found it less exacting to live in
the fifth or the thirteenth century may perhaps be
doubted. Distance lends enchantment to the view, and
many of the theological positions which we so readily
take for granted were the outcome of persistent thinking

[1] *Ecclesiastical Ballads*, II: Lilium Regis.

and rapier-like controversy. Where the present age probably differs from all previous periods in the Church's history is in the magnitude of the gap that yawns between the traditional outlook of the Church and the contemporary assumptions and evaluations of the society in which it lives. In consequence, quite apart from the novelty and intricacy of the questions that force themselves upon the Church's consciousness, there is a problem of communication of intimidating magnitude. It is not therefore surprising that some Christian writers and speakers have devoted so much attention to thinking as the contemporary world thinks that they have lost sight of the Gospel which the Church is commissioned to proclaim. It is possible to be so preoccupied in learning a language that one has no information to impart when one has learnt it. What use is the medium if one has no message? Furthermore, the fact that the contemporary world does not speak the Church's language may be a direct consequence of the fact that it has ignored or rejected the Church's message. If this is so, then we are not confronted simply with the task of learning the world's language and then seeing how much of the faith we can express in it; it may be necessary to teach the world a new language. True, we must have some acquaintance with the world's present language if we are to do this; in evangelisation the direct method has definite limitations. This does not alter the fact that it is the Church's language which we are to teach. And by "the Church's language" I do not simply mean the technical terms of theology; I mean the whole pattern of thought, the whole outlook upon reality and life, which the Church is commissioned to proclaim. There is a much-told story about the Irishman who, when asked the way to Roscommon, replied "If I wanted to get to Roscommon I wouldn't be starting from here." Nevertheless, starting from here – wherever "here" may happen to be – while it is a necessary, is not a sufficient, condition for getting to Roscommon. In his anxiety to be contemporary, the theologian is in grave danger of forgetting the truth on which I laid emphasis a few minutes ago, that the Church into whose membership the men and women of the present day are called consists not just of those Christians who are now on earth but of those who were once on earth and are now in heaven or in purgatory. Even considered as an earthly society the Church is a continuous and organically developing entity, whose history spans the ages, and if we refuse to take seriously the thought of our Christian past we shall cast away great treasures of wisdom and be left with nothing but the narrow and provincial outlook of the world of our own day from which to derive instruction and inspiration. Furthermore, our relation to the Church of the past is not merely that of accepting information and learning lessons from history. The Church's tradition is a great living inheritance of thought and life, most of whose content has hitherto been undiscerned and most of whose potentialities have hitherto been unactualised.

It is by bringing this great living inheritance into impact upon the world in which we live that our task towards that world will be achieved. This is a matter for great sensitivity, discernment and humility; it is not to be done by brutal and parrot-like repetition of the traditional formulas, without regard for the needs and condition of our hearers. We are perhaps unlikely to perform it with great success, but that is no reason for not performing it as successfully as we can. And we should remember that we are not dependent simply on our own resources, but on the grace of God. To speak of the Christian past as I have spoken is neither nostalgic nor romantic. As Karl Rahner has said, "The only defence of the inheritance of the past is the conquest of the future."[1] Nevertheless, to the conquest of the future we carry the whole armoury of our Christian past. Prophecy is notoriously unprofitable; Rahner reminds us of the example of "Gregory the Great, who himself was expecting the end of the world and yet became the father of the Middle Ages in the West."[2] What mattered was not Gregory's expectation but his fidelity. And it is perhaps to fidelity more than most other virtues that Christians in general and Christian theologians in particular are called today.

[1] *The Dynamic Element in the Church*, p. 4.
[2] ibid., p. 67.

THEOLOGY OF THE
SECULAR

Theology of the Secular

"IN ORDER TO BE EFFECTUAL IN THIS WORLD IT
is not enough to disbelieve in the other." These words,
which I quote from Dr Vigo A. Demant's penetrating
work *Religion and the Decline of Capitalism*,[1] will provide a
fitting introduction to the theme of this lecture. However, before I embark on this argument it will be
desirable to define carefully the precise meanings which
I propose to give to some of the terms which I shall use,
for they are in fact used by different writers in very different ways and neglect of this can only lead to confusion.

By "the secular", then, I shall mean that whole body
of human thought and action which is concerned solely
with "this world" and "this life", a life which for each
of us begins with the fertilisation of an ovum by a
spermatozoon and ends with bodily death. Thus I ex-
clude from the definition of "the secular" any concern
which a man may have with a possible future life and
any concern which he may have, even in "this life", with
an order of reality (if such there be) that transcends the
experience of the senses; this is the point of the word
"solely" in the last sentence. Thus the word "secular"
will be roughly synonymous with one of the uses of the
word "natural" by Christian theologians, namely that

[1] op. cit., p. 118.

use in which "natural" is contrasted with "super-natural". By "secularism" I shall mean the view that "the secular", as above defined, is the only reality that there is or at any rate the only reality of which human beings need to take account. As the adjective correlative to "secularism" I shall use the word "secularist", and this must be carefully distinguished from the ideologic-ally neutral adjective "secular".

Now one of the most obvious features of human his-tory during the last four centuries has been a colossal and unprecedented proliferation in the realm of the secular, a continually accelerating and, to all appear-ance, as yet unchecked development in man's under-standing and manipulation of the materials and the forces which go to make up "this world". This scientific and technological explosion has brought with it un-deniable, but not unmixed, blessings. Man has largely emancipated himself from his former subservience to the forces of nature and has brought them, at least potentially and in principle, under his own control, though it may well be doubted whether he has learnt how to exercise that control wisely and responsibly. It is, of course, easy to catalogue the items on the credit and debit sides of the account, though it is not so easy to decide at the end of the audit whether the account is in the black or the red; to balance the advances in medi-cine and surgery against the increase in psychological disorders, and the menace of nuclear warfare against the prospect of unlimited leisure and the joy of setting men upon the moon. I shall not indulge here in this pleasant arithmetical pastime. What I must stress, however, is that this proliferation of the secular has gone step by step with a parallel growth in secularism. The conjunction of the two is not altogether surprising, but it is certainly not logically or psychologically necessary. It is not surprising, because great success has an obvious tendency both to swell and to turn people's heads, and success in controlling the processes of nature can easily suggest that man is able by his own efforts to supply everything that he needs. But it is not logically or psychologically necessary, as can be seen from the fact that the great inaugurators of the scientific age were for the most part devout and intelligent Christians. It is nevertheless undeniable that the predominant mood in the technologically advanced communities today is secularist, whether the social structure is pluralist, as in the American and European democracies, or monolithic, as in the Soviet Union and China. Allowing for such partial exceptions as Spain and Ireland and for the backlog in the technologically more backward regions of Asia and Africa, it is broadly true that the modern world not only exhibits a vast proliferation in the realm of the secular but has in addition a thoroughly secularist outlook and behaves on thoroughly secularist assumptions. It organises itself in a way that takes no account of any other reality than that of "this world" and "this life".

In such a situation the Christian theologian cannot avoid asking himself what his concern and his attitude

L

should be. To use a modern cliché, what should be the "style" of theology in a secularist world? There is, as we well know, a vigorous and noisy group of writers who maintain that theology itself should become secularist, that its primary duty is to modify itself in accordance with the assumptions and aims of secularism where such modification is possible and to commit suicide where it is not. The Christian faith must be restated simply in terms of "this world", without any reference to a transcendent order of reality or to any life that may await us beyond the grave. Admittedly this is practically all that the members of this group have in common, apart from a contempt for traditional Christianity and a fondness for startling and provocative slogans. They range all the way from Dr John A. T. Robinson, for whom God undoubtedly exists but is best thought of as the Ground of being, to those who joyfully and triumphantly celebrate God's obsequies. And these latter, in their turn, range from moderates like Gabriel Vahanian, for whom the death of God signifies some kind of divine eclipse or withdrawal, to extremists like Thomas J. J. Altizer, according to whom God used to exist until he destroyed himself in order to emancipate man and for whom God was in any case identical with Satan. Indeed, Dr J. C. Cooper, in his book *The Roots of the Radical Theology*, has listed no fewer than ten distinct senses in which the Death of God is understood by different writers who announce it.[1]

[1] op. cit., pp. 31ff.

It is not my purpose here to castigate this particular *trahison des clercs* but to attempt a more constructive and rewarding task. Dr Ernest Gellner, in his book *Words and Things*, which enjoyed something of a *succès de scandale* on its publication in 1959, wrote: "A cleric who loses his faith abandons his calling, a philosopher who loses *his* redefines his subject",[1] but I think he might have reconsidered this judgment if he had been confronted with an avowedly atheistic theology. I will only enter a word of protest at this point against the practice of the writers whom I have in mind of appropriating to themselves a variety of laudatory epithets. "Honest", "candid", "courageous", "adult", "mature", "radical" – how familiar all these are, and what depths of cowardice, ignorance, wilful blindness, incompetence and superficiality they imply in those who venture to disagree with those who lay claim to them. "Do we begin", enquired the Apostle, "again to commend ourselves?" It will perhaps be a sufficient ambition for the Christian theologian if, abandoning aspiration for the more flamboyant virtues, he tries merely to say things that are relevant and true.

In place, then, of a secularist theology, which tries to bring itself into line with the outlook and aims of a secularised world, I wish to plead for a theology of the secular, by which I mean a branch of theology which will interpret the secular order, the things of "this world" and "this life", from the standpoint of Christian

[1]op. cit., p. 259.

belief, in order to enable Christians to live within it more intelligently and to influence it more effectively. There is indeed a vast body of Christian thinking, with its roots in the historic Christian tradition, that has been concerned with this task, though its existence is ignored by the secularist theologians. To give only two instances, it is exemplified in the Roman Communion by the great papal social encyclicals and the constitution *Gaudium et Spes* of Vatican II and in the Anglican Communion by the tradition of social thought and action typified by such names as F. D. Maurice, Charles Gore and William Temple.

Now clearly a theology of the secular must begin by considering the nature of the secular order itself. What, as Christianity sees it, is "this world", the world in which we are born, strive, love, hate, rejoice, sorrow and in the end die? If the Christian religion is true, the basic fact about it is that it is created by God; we must therefore begin by saying something about the Christian doctrine of creation.

Dr Harvey Cox has rightly pointed out that one of the great achievements of Judaeo-Christian religion has been to disenchant and de-divinise nature.[1] For primitive man, everything was living and divine, and, as M. Gilson has reminded us, even for such a comparatively sophisticated thinker as Thales, "all things are full of gods".[2] But what does this de-divinisation amount to? According to Dr Cox, "the Hebrew view of creation

---

[1] *The Secular City*, ch. i.   [2] *God and Philosophy*, ch. i.

(and this is, for him, also the Christian view of creation) separates nature from God and distinguishes man from nature", and he interprets this as meaning that nature has become absolutely, and not merely relatively, autonomous. Not only is nature not God, but it has no real relation to him. Everything in it happens as if God did not exist and, although man has been set over it as the Adam who is to mould it and transform it, he is to mould it and transform it as if God did not exist. "Yahweh, the Creator, whose being is centred outside the natural process, who calls it into existence and names its parts, allows man to perceive nature itself in a matter-of-fact way. . . . The mature secular man neither reverences nor ravages nature. His task is to tend it and make use of it, to assume the responsibility assigned to The Man, Adam."[1]

I believe that this view is mistaken on three counts. First of all, the Bible does not postulate such an extreme disconnectedness between God and nature as Dr Cox alleges. It does indeed make a radical distinction between God and nature and denies to nature any character of divinity. But what is this distinction? It is the distinction between Being that is altogether independent of the world and being that is entirely dependent upon God. Therefore, the very distinction between God and the world postulates that the world is not disconnected from God but is in the most intimate relation with him. It has indeed a relative autonomy, for God,

[1] op. cit., pp. 22f.

in making beings, makes real *beings*, although dependent ones, and not mere insubstantial phantoms. The creative act of God is not, as the eighteenth-century deists conceived it, a sheer *fiat* or command, which brought a world into existence and endowed it with certain principles of operation but had no further concern with it, rather like the politician of whom it was said that he could set his face talking and then go away and leave it. *Non enim fecit et abiit*, wrote St Augustine: "he did not make it and then go away". And the view of a God who is continually present to his creation, conserving it and energising it by his power, is not the fiction of a hellenising Christianity which has abandoned its biblical roots; it is the New-Testament teaching of a God without whom not one sparrow falls to the ground.

First, then, this doctrine of creation which Dr Cox proposes makes the wrong kind of separation of nature from God, But, secondly, it makes the wrong kind of distinction of man from nature. We have not told the truth about man when we have said that he is set over against nature and commissioned to tend it and make use of it. We must also remember – and the Bible, in contrast with Greek Platonism, is emphatic about this – that, on his physical and material side, man is continuous with nature and, indeed is literally part of it. Both his biological descent from pre-human stock and the facts of nutrition and excretion make this plain. In saying this, I am not denying by implication either the spirituality of man or his destiny beyond the grave;

there will be more to say about these later. But I am concerned to emphasise that man is a doubly constituted unity of body and soul, and that, through his bodily element, he is not simply a detached observer of the natural world but is also part of it.

Dr Cox himself does not seem to be particularly drawn towards the more existentialist types of philosophy, but it is in these that the detachment of man from nature receives its fullest expression. They are indeed determined to emphasise, and indeed to exaggerate, the fact of man's immersion in the natural world, but to be *in* something is not the same as to be *part* of it. The sense of disgust with his environment manifested by Antoine Roquentin in M. Sartre's novel *La Nausée* provides an example of this, but it is no less clear in the writing of the Christian existentialists, with their dependence on the thought of Martin Heidegger. For it is their constant concern to stress that man is not at home in the world but feels himself to be an alien. And if it be objected that Christian existentialists attribute this sense of alienation to man's sinfulness rather than to his creaturely status, two replies must be made: first, that existentialism, with its insistence on man's actual condition and its abhorrence of abstractions and hypothetical speculations, notoriously fails to make a clear distinction between man's creatureliness and his fallenness; and secondly, that the use of such words as *geworfen* to describe man's situation as one of being "hurled" into his environment plainly suggest that man is in no sense part of that environment. From this point of view, existentialism, except perhaps in the much qualified form in which we find it in such a writer as Dr John Macquarrie, would seem to be the worst possible philosophical system to adopt if one wishes to reconcile the scientific outlook with the Christian religion. Dr Ian G. Barbour, in his penetrating book *Issues in Science and Religion*, remarks that "although this method is valuable in representing the relation of man to God, it tends to bypass the problem of God's relation to nature – and in particular it says nothing about God's activity in nature."[1]

My third objection to Dr Cox's view of the secular order is that, while rightly de-divinising the natural world, it deprives the natural world of its true mystery and nobility. If the total truth about the natural world is simply that it is not God, it is emptied of all positive value and meaning. The naïve belief that everything is divine, which is ascribed, perhaps over-confidently, to primitive man, may be only a distortion of the very important truth that creatures embody and manifest, in their finite way, an analogical participation in the wonder and glory of God their Creator, who incessantly pours goodness into them: *infundens bonitatem in rebus*. "My love is as the hills", wrote St John of the Cross,

> The lonely valleys clad with forest-trees,
> The rushing, sounding rills,

[1] op. cit., p. 381; cf. pp. 431ff.

Strange isles in distant seas,
Lover-like whisperings, murmurs of the breeze.

Rare gifts he scatterèd
As through these woods and groves he pass'd apace,
Turning as on he sped
And clothing every place
With loveliest reflection of his face.[1]

If all that one can say as a theologian about the created world is comprised in the negative statement that the world is not divine, one will, I fear, be as unsuccessful in commending the Christian religion to the artist or the poet as to the scientist.

The doctrine that the whole fabric of created or secondary causality is perpetually upheld and energised by the primary causality of God does, of course, raise certain problems for the theologian. This in itself need give no cause for alarm; after all, if there were no theological problems remaining to be solved there would be no need for theologians. It was the difficulty of reconciling the activity of God with the deterministic universe of post-Newtonian physics that, as has been described by Dr Westfall and Dr Hurlbutt,[2] first of all confined God's activity to the first moment of the

[1] *Spiritual Canticle*, trans. E. Allison Peers.
[2] Richard S. Westfall, *Science and Religion in Seventeenth-Century England*; Robert H. Hurlbutt III, *Hume, Newton and the Design Argument*.

world's history and then pushed it over the horizon altogether. However, this particular difficulty is no longer present, since scientists have now abandoned the Newtonian determinism. It is sometimes alleged that in pointing to this fact one is indulging in the discreditable pastime of postulating a "God of the gaps". It must, however, be replied to this accusation that there is all the difference between confining God's activity to the gaps that science has not yet filled but has every hope of filling, and pointing to the fact that scientists themselves – or at any rate the dominant "Copenhagen" school – postulate these particular gaps as ultimate. But the real lesson to be learnt from this is that it is very unwise to clamp theology to *any* contemporary scientific view, whether superficially favourable or unfavourable to religion.

At the present time perhaps the most urgent topics for discussion arise out of the fact that science has now made it possible for man to manipulate and transform not only the world of which he is part but also that part of the world which is himself. The possibility, by microsurgical and other means, of bringing about radical modifications in human genetic material and in the neural material in which man's conscious and unconscious mental life appears to inhere raises novel and complex ethical problems for the scientist no less than for the theologian. This, I must emphasise, is not science-fiction; some of these things are happening already. The issues are far from clear, but it may well be that nothing less than the future of the human species is at stake. It may be extremely difficult to draw the line between the changes which would leave the essential nature of man intact and those which would change him into a different species altogether. It may be even more difficult to decide which changes, even among those which leave man's essence intact, are legitimate and desirable. And there will be burning questions as to the people in whose hands the decisions should lie. Both Christians and non-Christians will be faced with problems that they have never been faced with before. But it is clear that only a theology which takes full account of man's radical continuity with the rest of the physical universe on the material side of his being will be able even to enter into the discussion.

Nevertheless, imperative as it is to stress the material element in man's twofold nature, it is no less imperative to stress the spiritual element. If man is not an angel, neither is he a brute beast or a machine. Indeed it is precisely because man is the being in whom the realms of matter and spirit intersect and interpenetrate that the destiny of the whole material realm is implicated in the destiny of man. No one in our time has shown such an agonised concern with the worldly needs of mankind as Pope John XXIII, but no one has so clearly seen the impossibility of severing those worldly needs from man's supra-mundane destiny. To see this one need only read such a collection of his utterances as that which has been edited by Mgr Vincent A. Yzermans under the title *Pope John: Bailey Readings*. For John there was no question of choice, and still less of opposition, between the temporal and the eternal welfare of man, between his earthly and his heavenly concern. But this does not simply mean that the earthly life is something through which we must pass in order to reach our home in heaven and that if we are to reach that home we must be careful not to get lost on the way. In the mystery of our union with Christ we have already a foretaste of the goal. Furthermore, in the final consummation of the work of Christ the material world will have its share. This is the significance of the doctrine of the resurrection of the body.

The resurrection of the body has sometimes been interpreted as meaning simply that we shall be given in heaven some kind of quasi-physical organism which will take the place of the body which we left behind when we died but will have no organic connection with it. This I believe to be quite false, as false as the "angelism" which holds that our beatitude will involve our having no bodies at all. It is, of course, obvious that there can be no question of simply reassembling the material particles of which our bodies were composed either at the moment of death or at some earlier time. To think in that way would be to adhere unconsciously to a thoroughly outmoded view of matter which science itself has long abandoned. In whatever way we are to conceive the ultimate constitution of matter, whether as composed of centres of energy or as a pervasive field of gravitational and electromagnetic forces or in some other way still, it certainly is not made out of multitudes of impenetrable and indestructible particles whose only effect on one another is through elastic impact. The material realm is a great pattern of interacting and interweaving energies in which we ourselves are involved throughout our earthly lives. And although for each one of us there is an ever-changing, yet continuous and identifiable, sub-pattern which he knows as his "body", he is through that sub-pattern organically related to the pattern as a whole. How fundamentally our bodies are related to the rest of the realm of matter is plainly shown by such a familiar process as nutrition.

> Whatever Miss T. eats
> Turns into Miss T.

It has indeed been suggested, as by Fr Karl Rahner[1] and Fr Ladislaus Boros,[2] that at death the spiritual element in man does not lose all relation to matter but enters into some kind of wider relation with the whole material realm. If this is so, then the general resurrection will consist in a reorganisation of the material realm around these spiritual centres in such a way that the human race, having now reached its completion,

[1] K. Rahner, *On the Theology of Death.*
[2] L. Boros, *The Moment of Truth*, pp. 76ff.; *Pain and Providence*, pp. 44ff.

will be constituted as a perfectly functioning organic whole, integrated into the glorified humanity of Christ. Such a view seems to harmonise fully with, for example, the thought of St Paul. It may further be suggested that the character of the time-process, as subjectively experienced by any human spirit between death and resurrection, may be so different from that of any human being still in his earthly state that, for the former, the time may pass, as we should say, "in a flash". No scientist today, we may remind ourselves, looks upon time as one uniformly flowing stream, the same for every body in the universe.[1] (In passing it may be remarked that some of the problems raised by the doctrine of purgatory may find a solution here. Even in this earthly life, the lapse of time between two identifiable events such as the beginning and end of a cinema-show may be subjectively experienced very differently by two observers, one of whom is in a state of rapt attention and the other in a state of almost intolerable boredom.) Speculation of this kind is inevitably inconclusive, but it can lead to deeper understanding of the realities concerned, and it can also serve the useful purpose of demolishing objections based on outworn physical theories.

Man is, then, a psychophysical unity, a highly complicated and mysterious synthesis of body and soul, of matter and spirit, of two components which, while they are distinct from each other, are nevertheless genuinely

[1] Cf. e.g., G. J. Whitrow, *The Natural Philosophy of Time*, passim.

united to form one being and not two. Through his spiritual component man has a destiny lying beyond this world and this life. Through his material component his destiny is solidary with the destiny of the physical world, or, perhaps it would be more accurate to say, the destiny of the physical world is solidary with his. Through the real union of the two components man is the meeting-place through which the physical realm itself is to be gathered into his own transcendent destiny; the resurrection of the body, of which the Creed speaks, is at the same time the transfiguration and transformation of the material realm, the *anakephalaiōsis* or gathering up of all things in the risen Christ to which the Epistle to the Ephesians bears witness.[1]

I have insisted at, I fear, wearisome length on this twofold, and at the same time unitary, nature of man because there is an ever-present danger that one or other of the components will be virtually ignored. There is a parallel here with the doctrine of the person and natures of Christ himself; indeed the document called the Creed of St Athanasius explicitly says that, as a rational soul and flesh make one man, so God and man make one Christ. And just as an unbalanced stress on either the godhead or the manhood in Christ leads to the Eutychian or the Nestorian heresy respectively, so an unbalanced stress on either the soul or the body in man leads either to the angelism for which this world has no real importance or to the

[1] Eph. i. 10.

secularism for which man is entirely a denizen of this world and has no destiny beyond this life.

There are, of course, a great many aspects of man which an adequate theology of the secular will have to discuss. Each human being – each psychophysical unity and unit – is not an isolated and incapsulated ego but a member of the total human race and of the various communities within it. Just as, through his physical metabolism, a human being is inherent in the world of matter, so through his powers of communication and co-operation he is inherent in the human community and its various sub-communities. Furthermore, by the sexual differentiation of the human species human beings are involved in the whole complex of man/woman relationships, and, by the way in which sexual differentiation is linked with the procreation and nurture of the young, they are involved in the complex of family life. It is impossible to do more than mention these here but there is one essential fact which I must emphasise in this context.

The Christian revelation, while it provides us with the basic truths about the nature, destiny, condition and resources of man, tells us very little about their details. God has paid us the compliment of leaving us to find out these for ourselves with the aids which he gives us. Therefore the Christian theologian should respect and encourage the rightful autonomy of the various positive sciences which are concerned, whether proximately or remotely, with human life and welfare:

biology, psychology, sociology and, where they are relevant, even chemistry and physics. As a matter of history the Church has done this very whole-heartedly and indeed some of our present problems arise precisely from this. Theologians such as St Thomas Aquinas accepted with the greatest respect everything that the secular science of the time told them about man and the universe and, while theoretically holding that scientific theories were subject to correction, incorporated them very thoroughly into their theological systems. Our present difficulty arises from the fact that the science of the ancient and the medieval world was at best incomplete and provisional and at worst downright erroneous. We are therefore faced today with the tremendous task, which we have only just begun to attempt, of eliminating these outworn scientific theories and replacing them by those of the present day. We have to assimilate into theology the discoveries and perspectives of modern science as our predecessors assimilated those of the science of their day. But here some caution must be observed.

The sciences of today are far more specialised than were those of the past. It is no longer possible for theologians simply to read the scientific text-books and popular expositions and then to incorporate as much of their contents as they have understood into the fabric of theology. The task can be done only by carefully planned and carefully conducted co-operative discussion in groups, some of which will be of very limited

M

range, in which theologians meet their secular col-
leagues on terms of mutual respect and understanding.
The keynote must be that of dialogue, not of debate. A
number of such groups, convoked either for specific
issues of immediate importance or for continuing discourse, have already come into being in various places,
but there is need for many more.

There is a further point which needs stressing, though
it will be unpopular in some circles. In spite of its
stupendously successful career and the unprecedented
revolution which it has brought about in human thinking and living, science as we now conceive it must not
be looked on as eternal and absolute. When some long-
standing and deeply rooted system which in its time had
seemed to be to all intents and purposes eternal has
been overthrown and its place taken by another, the
human mind has a strange tendency to ascribe to the
new system the character of absoluteness and eternality
which had been mistakenly ascribed to the old. This is
indeed surprising, for the correct lesson to be learnt
might surely be that *all* systems in the particular field
are relative and provisional, the new no less than the
old. Thus when we compare the vast range of achievement of modern science in the realm of discovery and
technology with the tiny and limited achievements of
earlier times, it might seem natural not to conclude that
future developments will take place by an indefinite
extension and proliferation along the lines that have
now established themselves, but rather to suspect that a

totally new kind of insight into the nature of created being may one day be discovered, as a result of which man's understanding of the world and his control over its forces may exceed his present achievements as much as, or perhaps far more than, his present achievements exceed those of classical antiquity and the Middle Ages. Neither the certainty of such a transformation can be affirmed nor its character predicted, but its possibility should be recognised. If this speculation seems utterly fantastic, it may be salutary to put ourselves in imagination in the position of a thoughtful and educated citizen of the Roman Empire in the fifth century, or of England in the thirteenth, or of the United States in the eighteenth, and then ask ourselves what we should expect the world to be like towards the end of the twentieth. This is not science-fiction, for science-fiction merely extrapolates as far as possible along the existing lines of development; this is something far more advanced and revolutionary, which cannot yet be written. The one thing that we can say about it is that, in so far as it is in accordance with reality, it will not contradict the Christian revelation. There will be plenty of work for theologians to do. But they will be placed at a serious disadvantage if they inherit from us a theological system which is as intricately entangled with the scientific outlook of the twentieth century as the theological systems which we have inherited have been entangled with the scientific outlook of the pre-Copernican age. Theology must always be sensitive to the out-

look of its time, and should concern itself with contemporary needs and problems, but it should never place all
its eggs in the contemporary basket, or, to change the
metaphor, put its shirt on the contemporary horse.

We must now ask the question how a theology of the
secular will envisage the task not merely of the theologian but of the ordinary man – and in particular the
Christian man – who is concerned with the day-by-day
affairs of the secular world. What has a theology of the
secular to say about man's concern with the secular?
In the light of the previous discussion the answer should
be clear. Man – man in Christ, man in whom the heal-
ing and transforming grace of God is already at work –
is to be the instrument and the agent through whom the
transfiguration of the world, the gathering up of all
things in Christ, is to be achieved. Not only the great
and impressive organisations for human welfare and
progress, but the conscientious work of every individual
man and woman, if it is offered to God by each according to the light which he has received, is the transfiguration of that small bit of the created world in which
his life and work is set. It is an element in the one great
process of restoration and fulfilment which will reach its
climax and perfection at the Last Day, when Christ will
deliver up the kingdom to God the Father, and God will
be all in all.[1] Pope Pius XI, in his encyclical *Quadragesimo Anno* in 1931, lamented a situation in which
dead matter left the factory ennobled and transformed

[1] I Cor. xv. 24, 28.

while men were corrupted and degraded.[1] But the true ennoblement and transformation of matter will be one in which man himself is ennobled and transformed, and indeed it can be brought about only by man who is himself ennobled and transformed in Christ by the grace of God. The transformation of man and of matter, the transformation of individual men and of human society, the transformation of man in the Church and the transformation of the human race by the Church, all these must go together, for they are parts of one great process of Christification.

Once again, there are a host of questions for a theology of the secular which I can only mention in passing. The fact that man is fallen and that, as fallen, he cannot be transformed without being redeemed and restored; the way in which purely secular organisations and activities for human welfare can be the instruments and agents of a God to whom they are often indifferent or even hostile; the relation between the Church and the world, considered not as two great power-complexes, but rather as the leaven and the bread which, when leavened, is to be the food of man; the type and method of prayer which is possible and fruitful for people living under the conditions of modern life – all these, considered not merely as theoretical problems to exercise the ingenuity of academic theologians but in the context of the lives of twentieth-century men and women, old and young, intelligent and stupid, favoured

[1] *Quadragesimo Anno*, Cath. Truth Soc. ed., p. 62.

and under-privileged, black, yellow and white – all these will fall within the ambit of a relevant theology of the secular. But behind all these there lies one basic truth about created being in general and man in particular without which any theological discussion of the secular order inevitably becomes either one-sided or incoherent. This is the truth of the fundamental *openness* of all finite being, and it sharply distinguishes the Christian view of the finite world and its components from the closed view which was characteristic of pre-Christian classical philosophy.

For pre-Christian philosophy every being was envisaged as a rounded off and sealed up entity, which contained within itself in potentiality everything that it could ever possibly become, although which of the potentialities were in fact actualised would very largely depend on the outside influences which bore upon it. In contrast to this fundamentally static view, the Christian religion holds that finite beings, just because they are held in existence by God from moment to moment, are essentially open to fresh influxes of divine power and love. Because they are perpetually open to God their future can never be fully predicted. We can be sure that God will not act upon them in a way which would contradict or destroy the nature he has already given them, but we cannot predict the precise ways in which he may amplify and transform it. And it is against the background of this view of finite beings that we must understand the traditional Christian doctrine that grace does not destroy nature but perfects it. The supernatural order into which man is elevated by grace does not remove man from the natural order, nor does it slam on to the top of his nature a supernatural slab, nor does it suppress nature in order to make room for itself. Grace does not merely perfect nature, it also presupposes it and cannot do without it.[1] It is quite wrong to think that grace is a kind of supernatural substance and that nature exists for the sake of it. On the contrary, grace apart from nature is a pure abstraction; and it is for the sake of nature that grace exists. Supernature simply means nature supernaturalised by grace, and the possibility of this supernaturalisation lies in the openness of nature to God. For a nature which was closed in the pre-Christian sense, supernaturalisation would be identical with destruction, for it could only mean the replacement of one nature by another. But for a nature which is open in the Christian sense, supernaturalisation means expansion, development, perfection, a realisation of hitherto unsuspected potentialities, a new infusion of the creative activity of God; and when supernaturalisation has taken place unlimited possibilities of further supernaturalisation lie ahead. In each stage of the process God takes the initiative; the creature can neither envisage what the next stage will be, nor demand its fulfilment as a right, nor initiate its achievement.

[1] Cf. St Thomas Aquinas, *Summa Theologiae*, I, i, 8 *ad* 2; I, ii, 2 *ad* 1.

Nevertheless, as the process goes on the creature finds its own activity not by-passed or suppressed, but on the contrary liberated and enhanced. The more it is super-naturalised, the more truly natural it becomes. And all this because openness to God is of its very essence; dependence on him is part of its definition. Supernature and nature, grace and human freedom, these are organically related in the dealings of God with man.[1]

These, then, as I see the matter, are some of the features of a theology of the secular, but this discussion cannot claim to be in any degree complete. There is indeed no doctrine of the Christian faith which will not have some part to play in a theology of the secular. Nevertheless, two points will, I hope have become clear. The first is that a theology of the secular is almost the precise contrary of a secularist theology. The second is that a theology of the secular ascribes to the secular a dignity and offers it a hope that a secularist theology is powerless to provide. The basic problem of contemporary man is how he can look the facts of his situation honestly in the face without falling into either cynicism or despair. Man who knows that he is made by God and redeemed by Christ can confront the facts without fear. I will conclude this lecture by quoting two passages from Christian writers, widely separated in time if not in faith.

In Clive Staples Lewis's novel *Prince Caspian*, the

[1] Most of this paragraph is taken from my book *The Importance of Being Human*, pp. 61f.

great lion Aslan, who is a symbol of the incarnate Lord Christ, bids farewell to the little group of human children in these words: "You come of the Lord Adam and the Lady Eve. And that is both honour enough to erect the head of the poorest beggar, and shame enough to bow the shoulders of the greatest emperor on earth. Be content."[1]

The other quotation is from St Augustine: "We have begun to be some great thing. Let no man despise himself. We were once nothing, but we are something. . . . We have said, 'Remember that we are dust'; but out of the dust he made man, and to dust he gave life, and in Christ he hath brought this dust to the kingdom of heaven, he who made heaven and earth."[2]

[1] op. cit., ch. xv.
[2] quoted by Alfred Noyes, *The Unknown God*, p. 251.